HAMPDEN BABYLON

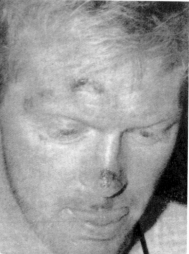

HAMPDEN BABYLON

SEX AND SCANDAL IN SCOTTISH FOOTBALL

STUART COSGROVE

CANONGATE

First published in Great Britain in 1991 by Canongate Books
This revised and updated edition published 2001
10 9 8 7 6 5 4 3 2 1

BRITISH LIBRARY CATALOGUING-IN-PUBLICATION DATA
A catalogue record for this book is available on request from the British Library
ISBN 1 84195 196 X

PHOTOGRAPH ACKNOWLEDGMENTS
The publishers gratefully acknowledge permission granted from the following sources for the right to reproduce photographs in *Hampden Babylon*: *Glasgow Herald*, Mirror Syndication International, PA Photos

Typesetting and design by Forge Design www.forgedesign.co.uk
Printed and bound by Butler & Tanner

www.canongate.net

CONTENTS

1

RAMON VEGA SUPERSTAR

(HE LOOKS LIKE A MODEL AND HE WEARS A BRA)

Football is not really a sport, it is a vapour; part of the air we breathe. I have tried to imagine a life without it, a history devoid of of Mo Johnston. An upbringing in which Champagne Charlie never existed. A life without the comic catchphrase "Where's the Burdz?" I have tried to imagine a history cleansed of trips to Wembley, and conversations about wine that don't stray with inevitable logic back to Buckfast, away games at Airdrie – and Section B.

Football is a virus. It is the disease we have contracted as punishment for being Scots.

There are numerous ways that we can make sense of the popular obsession with football: to describe it as religion, a culture and – in the wake of the Ibrox disaster, Heysel, Bradford and Hillsborough – even as a form of tragedy, a game that insists on ending in human suffering. But each grand pattern for football stumbles on a joke, those

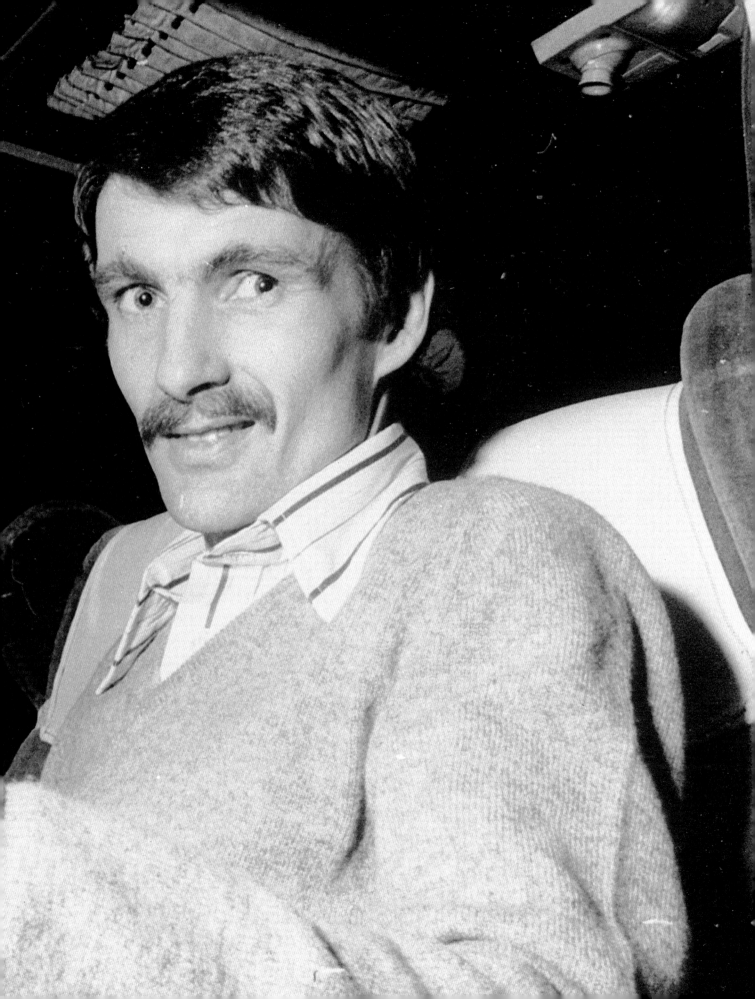

Darling, I have simply *nothing* to wear to Brockville. Vega and Westwood discuss tactics

inevitable one-liners that keep football fans amused and spread diseased humour around the terraces. Football humour is the best testament to the resilience of the game, proof that it is alive with a cruel imagination.

My favourite jokes are inevitably about football in Scotland, a nation where the game has an extra layer of significance. We have all tried to picture a scene in which a bitter Rangers fan returns home to find his wife arranging a display of dried flowers. Angry at her insensitivity he throws a vase at the flock wallpaper and shouts: "I've told you Effie. No pot-pourri here!"

No popery here? Only in Scotland could an amateur Polish goalkeeper turned Pontiff and a bunch of dried flowers meet in such painful wordplay.

Scottish football occupies its own peculiar universe, a place populated by losers, boozers and substance-abusers.

The Scottish footballer is traditionally an antihero; a player whose flawed personality teeters on the brink of self-destruction. Whatever our nearest neighbours, the English, think about Scottish football – dodgy keepers, pissed-up ball players, cheap transfers – they are almost inevitably wrong. The truth is considerably darker, almost satanic.

Hampden Babylon is a home for the wayward – it is the door where genius nearly knocked. It always bids a fond welcome to scandal whether it is Mo Johnston's controversial transfer to Rangers or Charlie Cooke's scandal of the vodka dollies. It is the home of truly remarkable characters, some flawed, some farcical.

There is Chic Charnley, the one-time Partick Thistle midfielder, a man of mesmerising skills who showed utter contempt for the real world. A playmaker in the mould of Zidane, he attracted trouble like a magnet. At a ramshackle training session at Thistle's training ground in Glasgow's Maryhill, what passed as a tactics session turned sour when a local gang wielding swords attacked Chic for some long-forgotten grievance, a dispute over money, women or turf. Rather than protect himself, Chic led his team mates in a counter attack that would have shamed the Zulu nation.

Then there was St Mirren's Barry Lavety, the first victim of football's rave generation. He admitted taking Ecstasy at a Saltcoats club and was forced to atone on the pages of Scotland's daily papers. Such was the moral panic around drugs at a time when hundreds of young people had died that the player was forced to undergo a humiliating period of rehab in a clinic in the Borders. "I'm not sure Lavety's back to full fitness," a joker of the time said. "Every time the ref blows the whistle Lavety shouts 'Acieeeed'."

The arrival of imported foreigners from around the world may threaten the development of indigenous youth and the quality of the national team, but it has not stemmed the flow of eccentrics who have chosen Scotland as their home and football as their trade.

Take Pasquale Bruno, the Mafia don who played for Hearts. One of the first imports from Italy's notorious Serie A, Pasquale was a fierce-tackling defender whose notoriety was bound up in national stereotypes. Football fans immediately cast him as a Mafia godfather picking the team, deciding tactics and orchestrating substitutions.

According to legend, anyone who disagreed with the don woke up with a severed horse's head in his bed, or rather a severed donkey's head. The donkey was invariably Pasquale's team mate, Dave McPherson.

It would be tempting to do a pretentious detour and describe the cast of characters in Scottish footballers as Rabelaisian or better still compare them to robust characters who populate the poems of Rabbie Burns: flawed, earthy and unconditionally human.

Scottish culture has wrestled for centuries to find ways of representing the national condition – the economic collusions that bind us to England, the tangled sectarianism that binds us to Ireland, and the national schizophrenia that binds us to our fractured self.

21st century boy

The hunt has often taken us through the maze of football. But not even Sigmund Freud, the most eminent psychoanalyst of the twentieth century, could adequately explain Scotland, or indeed why Celtic defender Ramon Vega paraded down a fashion catwalk in Milan wearing a grey miniskirt.

Ramon's greatest moment came strutting in front of the fashion cognoscenti in a manner my Uncle Billy, a philosopher of the old school, accurately described as a "total Jessie".

Vega's stay in Scotland was short but instructive about the ways football is changing. He is a product of football in the first days of the 21st century: a modern, wealthy and 'feminised' player. Here is a man who turns up at training on time, has his own agent, a personal website and eats pasta in order to maximise his athletic performance.

Vega is a lesser contemporary of the ultimate feminised footballer, England and Manchester United star, David Beckham – a man who wears a sarong, spends more on face cream than most people earn in a week, and who takes an active role in child-rearing.

Football players increasingly see themselves as actors in a drama who deserve the benefits of the performing arts. But there was one funamental flaw. Unfortunately for Vega his audience was comprised of football fans, most of whom are still struggling to

He strutted in a manner my Uncle Billy, a philosopher of the old school, once described as a "total Jessie"

leave the values of the previous century behind.

His decision to wear a miniskirt was taken in the past, before his career brought him to one of life's leading moral backwaters – Scotland. How Vega must have regretted wearing a frock when he was trying to defend a corner on a freezing cold afternoon at Tynecastle. Hearts fans are not generous when it comes to haute couture or hemlines. How he must have regretted that particular shade of grey when his back was to the massed ranks of Killie fans at Rugby Park. The wolf whistles must have cut him to the quick.

How Vega must wish he could wind back the clock. But none of us can.

Football has changed forever. And the values that shaped its development in the twentieth century are fast disappearing. The shipyards that produced Alex Ferguson are closing down. The mines that gave us Jock Stein and Matt Busby have already gone and heavy industrial monuments like Ravenscraig have been pulled own.

Footballers were once the local stars of industrialism. Their direct route out

of the graft and toil of hard work was a contract with a professional club or a steam train south to England, where they could ply their trade alongside hundreds of other talented Scots.

Hughie Gallacher, Alex James and Denis Law all made the journey south, not really knowing if they were bound to be legends or losers. But they could be sure of one thing; once they arrived in England they would be surrounded by people like themsleves – working class Scots whose talent stood out in the crowd and whose disposition for mayhem and misbehaviour was the stuff of football notoriety.

The journey of Scottish football, from hard-men to hemlines, is long and eventful. Like the nativity, it began in a manger, this time in Bellshill in the year 1903. An infant baby was born and his name was Hughie. Sadly they couldn't find a virgin for miles and the only person at the birth who could be described as miraculous was a drunken neighbour.

This is the story of a country and uncurable condition.

This is Hampden Babylon. ◊

2

GALLACHER'S LAST GOODBYE

Drink, drugs, sex and scandal are part of the fabric of Scottish football, but remarkably, in the entire history of the game, only one player has stood accused of being drunk in charge of a football. His name was Hughie Gallacher.

Gallacher was the personification of the Babylonian art of scandal. Throughout his brilliant career with Airdrie, Newcastle, Chelsea and Derby, controversy pursued him like a faithful dog. The headlines of his life read like a draft-script of the tempestuous

Scottish footballer. Troubled by a broken marriage, bankruptcy, a drink problem and inflamed by a wild and uncontrollable temper, he was football's answer to Benny Lynch, a genius in search of tragedy.

Hughie Gallacher was born in 1903 in Bellshill, Lanarkshire, one of the deprived academies of football excellence in turn-of-the-century Scotland. His father was an Ulsterman who emigrated to Scotland to work in the mines. He married a local woman and presided over a strictly Protestant household in which both parents were active members of the Orange Lodge.

Despite his Protestant upbringing, Gallacher and his teenage schoolfriend, the legendary Alex James of Arsenal and Scotland, were fanatical Celtic fans. At 16 Gallacher signed for Tannochside Athletic, a Lanarkshire juvenile team and barely a year later he married a Catholic girl, Annie

McIlvaney, crossing the divide and causing untold disputes within his family.

The marriage was a mistake. The couple stayed together for little more than a year and their infant son died before he was 12 months old, an incident that was to haunt Gallacher throughout his precociously successful playing career.

After a spell with Queen of the South, Gallacher moved to Airdrieonians to become a vital part of the club's famous Scottish Cup

The clothes were a prop and according to his team mates the money was made of carefully clipped strips of newspaper

"Don't call me scarface"

winning team of 1924.

Gallacher set the rules for all that was to follow in Hampden Babylon. Only five foot two inches tall, he turned his diminutive height into an abrasive asset, wriggling through towering defenders in the old 'tanner ba' tradition. The sight of his small and snake-like frame weaving through packed defences virtually established the image of the tiny and recalcitrant Scottish forward, a mantle that was to be worn with tetchy and attitudinal

pride by successors like Willie Henderson, Jimmy Johnstone, Gordon Strachan, David Speedie and Mo Johnston.

In one season alone Gallacher scored 46 goals for Airdrie, striking up an almost telepathic relationship with the club's left winger, Jimmy Sommerville, a name that conjures up images of late 1980s gay disco rather than Broomfield Park in the midst of industrial depression.

King of the hat-tricks

In the mid-Twenties Gallacher established himself as Scotland's first-choice striker and ultimately became the only Scottish international to score four hat-tricks for his country. Those of us raised on the gruel of modern Scotland can only marvel at the very thought of a hat-trick – let alone four.

Such was Gallacher's prowess that he once scored five goals in a 7–3 victory against Ireland. At half-time a note was passed to the Scottish dressing room telling the young striker that he would be shot if he did not ease off in the second half. Gallacher ignored the threats, played a blinder, then woke the next day with the intention of visiting friends in Belfast. As he passed by the city's Queen's Bridge a bullet ricocheted off a nearby wall as the Scottish internationalist dived for cover. To this day the incident has never been fully explained – a lone gunman on the grassy knoll or a major conspiracy of the state? But when Hughie was in town these kinds of things just happened.

It was with Newcastle United that the legend of 'Wee Hughie' was born. In the true spirit of a scandalous soccer star, Gallacher was flamboyant and temperamental on and off the park.

Like so many footballers after him, Gallacher was idolised in the working men's clubs of Newcastle and delighted his fans by flaunting his style. Dressed in fashionable double-breasted suits, white spats, a gangster's hat and a rolled umbrella, Gallacher projected the image of a dandy and a desperado. He frequently waved wads of money at passers-by but like most footballers of his era Gallacher was never really a rich man. The clothes were a prop and according to his team mates the money was made of carefully clipped strips of newspaper. Hughie was a poseur of uncontrollable proportions.

Gallacher made 174 league appearances for Newcastle, steering them to an English League Championship victory as captain in 1927 and eventually amassing 143 goals for the club. At the basis of his outrageous talent – and inevitably the root of his temperamental insecurities – was his diminutive height and the almost vindictive treatment he received at the feet of bigger and stronger opponents.

The Scottish goalkeeper Jack Harkness once claimed, "I never saw any forward with as many scars and hacks." Gallacher's brother-in-law, the Gateshead player George Mathieson, remembered: "You had to see his legs to believe the treatment he was given.

Hughie Gallacher: At war with authority

haviour that was to drive a wedge between Gallacher and the unfortunate clubs who tried to tame his wayward spirit.

We'll deport you evermore

At the height of his career, Gallacher played at Wembley in Scotland's famous 1928 victory over England. Although he broke his regular Saturday habit and failed to score, two of Hughie's former Bellshill school-friends, Alex James and Alex Jackson, scored five in a breathtaking display of unfettered Scottish football. Throughout the history of the miserable game, this match will stand out above all others as the day we actually got it right.

The victory was magically achieved by a forward line of five irrepressible midgets who are etched in history as 'The Wembley Wizards'. The Tartan Army, Scotland's swaggering support, can only drool at the thought of the match. Not only did Scotland get it right up them; they did it with midgets. If the years of poverty, scurvy and infant mortality that gripped Lanarkshire ever delivered a day in the sun it was in 1928 at a stadium hundreds of miles away in London.

Ironically, Gallacher's capacity for tragedy did not leave him for long; at the end of his most famous game he was told that his sister-in-law had died in Scotland. As the bedraggled Scotland fans led a ragtime jazz-band through the streets of London, celebrating the greatest victory in the history of Scottish football, Hughie Gallacher was on his way home to the funeral.

Like many of his compatriots in the rogues gallery of Scottish football, Hughie Gallacher compulsively disliked authority. He treated the club directors with withering contempt, and he had a life-long battle with the disciplinarians of the English Football

They were pitted, scarred. You couldn't blame him for losing his cool."

Hughie Gallacher specialised in losing his cool.

His disciplinary record was appalling and in modern times only Willie Johnston of Rangers, Billy Bremner of Leeds and the legendary Chic Charnley of Partick Thistle come remotely close to seizing his crown. Soon after he met his second wife, Hannah Anderson, a publican's daughter from Gateshead, Gallacher was arrested for brawling with her brother under Newcastle's High Level Bridge. Both men were bound over to keep the peace, but the incident was the beginning of a long history of misbe-

League. But like so many inspired players he reserved his deepest loathing for referees, that brotherhood of unfortunates whose eyesight, parenthood and denominational faith are the subjects of weekly abuse up and down the country.

Although he was born in the country that begat Tom 'Tiny' Wharton, Andrew Waddell and Hugh Dallas, Gallacher focused his venom on a famous English referee, Bert Fogg. The vendetta came to a head on New Year's Eve 1927, a few months before the Wembley Wizards destroyed England.

In a home match against Huddersfield Town, Newcastle were 3–2 down after conceding a questionable penalty to the visitors. Gallacher led the Newcastle protests, which increased in their ferocity after he was pulled down in the box and denied the penalty that would level the score. The incidents that followed border on the absurd and contradict

Gallacher and his wife

the nostalgic fallacy that footballers of the past played in gentlemanly accord with the rules.

Irritated by Gallacher's perpetual arguing, the referee threatened to book the Scottish striker. When he was asked his name, Gallacher replied with typical arrogance, "If you don't know me, you've no business being on the field! And what's your name?" Clearly taken aback by the striker's impudence, the referee replied "I'm Mr Fogg," to which Gallacher speedily retorted "Aye, and you've been in one all afternoon."

If the dispute had ended there, the exchange of words would have been a forgotten anecdote in football folklore. But the bad boy from Bellshill had only just begun.

In with the bathwater

Gallacher continued to argue with the referee throughout the game and followed him off the pitch at the end wagging his finger in the official's face. When the temperature cooled down a few minutes later Gallacher headed to the referee's dressing room to apologise. As he opened the door he saw the official, stripped naked, leaning over the bath. It was a moment of such farcical proportions that Gallacher could not resist. He kicked the unfortunate Fogg, propelling him head first into the bath. The English FA took a draconian view of what was described as Gallacher's "improper conduct" and he was suspended without pay for two months, the first man in professional football to be charged with kicking a

referee into a bath. Latter-day miscreants such as Paolo Di Canio could only marvel at such a charge.

It was on an overseas tour with Newcastle that Gallacher earned the dubious notoriety of being the first player to be accused of being drunk in charge of a football. In May 1929, Newcastle United played a series of European games in Italy, Czechoslovakia, Hungary and Austria.

The tour was a disaster. Newcastle lost by two goals to Ambrosiana, the team that eventually transformed into Inter Milan, and were thrashed 8–1 by the crack Czech team FC Slovak. By the time they arrived in Budapest to play a Hungarian select, the Magpies had lost interest and were beaten 4–1 in what by all accounts was more like a pitched battle than a football match.

Newcastle's full-back Maitland was sent off, followed almost inevitably by Gallacher after a fight with a Hungarian player. As he headed for the sanctuary of the dressing room, accompanied by armed soldiers, the home fans spat, threw coins and jeered at the tiny Scot.

After the game, Hungarian officials lodged a complaint against the Newcastle team, specifically Gallacher, accusing them of being drunk and disorderly. The appearance money due to Newcastle was withheld. Gallacher was on the verge of being deported, and the team returned to England to face a full enquiry at the English FA Headquarters in Lancaster Gate.

Gallacher claimed at the enquiry that he and his team mates had been thirsty prior to the game, and rinsed their mouths out with whisky and water. The football authorities in England accepted the explanation and sided with Gallacher and the Newcastle team, probably as a gesture of national protocol rather than with the conviction that the Scot was telling the truth.

The FA took a draconian view of Gallacher's "improper conduct" and he was the first man in professional football to be charged with kicking a referee into a bath

Overdressed to kill

Something in the genetic code of the family Gallacher seems to trigger scandal. If Hughie Gallacher was the first Scot to be accused of being drunk in charge of a football then his namesake, Patsy Gallacher, had already gone one better.

Very few transvestites have actually played for Scotland. Or at least admitted it. Patsy Gallacher remains one of the very few sexual renegades who have dared to parade around in women's clothes in front of their team mates.

Patsy was a ship-builder, who played for Celtic when they were a dominant force in Scottish football, in the first decade of the century. He was one of the smallest players in the game and was known throughout his career as 'The Mighty Atom', a tribute to his size, speed and power.

At the height of Celtic's success, the club's manager Willie Maley took his team to a luxury hotel in Dunbar for a period of training and relaxation. Even in the infant days of Scottish football, managers had realised the wisdom of a night-time curfew, and Gallacher and his team mates were given strict instructions to remain in the hotel.

In what must rank as one of the most ingenious ruses in the history of Hampden Babylon, Patsy Gallacher struck up a relationship with the hotel chambermaid and borrowed her clothes for the night.

So, dressed in a maid's outfit and disguised by a black veil, he wiggled through reception, bidding the club's manager goodnight in a high-pitched voice. Willie Maley, a pearl among swine, dutifully held the door open for the departing damsel. It was weeks later before he realised that it was one of his players, heading for a dram in Dunbar High Street.

None of Scotland's famous disciplinarian managers – Jock Stein, Alex Ferguson or Dundee United's Jim McLean – have ever had to confront such a complicated managerial problem. Admittedly Ferguson has had to suffer the effrontery of watching David Beckham in an Asian sarong – but a veil, nylons and a chambermaid's outfit?

Patsy Gallacher went on to play for Celtic for 15 years and scored the winning goal in their famous Cup-winning side of 1925, when he beat the entire Dundee defence and somersaulted into the net with the ball between his feet.

If Patsy had a penchant for a pretty frock, Hughie Gallacher had a drink problem. He was a long way from being an alcoholic, but he was vulnerable to heavy social drinking and was a sucker for the old Scottish adage 'One for the Road'. During his period at Newcastle and later in his career when he briefly played for Grimsby Town, Gallacher was known to drink with fans in pubs near the ground, and on more than one occasion a search party had to be sent to get him in time for the kick-off.

It is reassuring to know that Gallacher was one of the players chosen to represent Scotland when the national team played its first overseas international against France in May 1930. The team included two of Gallacher's favourite sparring partners, the Huddersfield Town winger Alec Jackson and Aberdeen's bustling striker Alec Cheyne. Neither could be described as a sobering influence.

One of the cardinal rules of Hampden Babylon is that curfews are made to be broken and managers are born to be duped. In a premonition of things to come, the team was placed under strict instructions to be in bed early the night before the game.

Knowing that Scottish footballers were in town, the Moulin Rouge warmed up for a busy night, and predictably Gallacher led a rabble of players through a hotel window to the forbidden pleasures of Parisian life. Scotland won 2–0, the offending players were censured, and the ritual of the broken curfew began its long and illustrious career as one of Scottish football's lasting contributions to the game.

Later that month, the former Rangers and Scotland forward Andy Cunningham was appointed manager of Newcastle and although he had played alongside Gallacher in the Scotland team a few years before, there was no great bond between the two. "Once Cunningham arrived as boss," Hughie once said, "I knew my days were numbered." The two players

Gallacher: a microcosm of future scandals

Knowing that Scottish footballers were in town, the Moulin Rouge warmed up for a busy night

came from different sides of the Scottish footballing psyche.

Gallacher was a renegade, a prototype of the Scottish Babylonian, a skilful but troublesome footballer always at war with the world and who always exercised his constitutional right to be 'gallus'. He was the natural ancestor of Jim Baxter, Jimmy Johnstone and Ally McCoist and the rogues or rascals who followed them into Scotland shirts.

Cunningham was a rationalist, a member of that more stern, censorious and dour breed that was to produce disciplinarian managers like Bill Struth of Rangers, Jock Stein of Celtic and the Brothers Glum – Tommy and Jim McLean.

At the dark heart of Scottish football, there is a titanic struggle between wild men and disciplinarians, between renegades and rationalists, between Jekyll and Hyde. It is a struggle for psychological supremacy that would be played out again and again as the twentieth century unwound. This time

discipline won and Hughie Gallacher was transferred south to Chelsea. But if discipline won the battle, the war was far from over.

Smoke gets in your eyes

London had never witnessed a footballer quite like Hughie Gallacher. In his opening game he scored twice in a 6–2 victory over Manchester United and continued to score with astounding regularity throughout the season.

His encounters off the field became even more dramatic. He was arrested for disorderly conduct after a fight with a gang of Fulham fans outside a café in London's Waltham Green. On another occasion he was spotted by an opposing Derby County player lying drunk in the street the night before an important league match, a scene that he repeated on several occasions in London's late-night jazz clubs.

In 1932, Gallacher had been joined at Chelsea by his two fellow internationalists, Jackson and Cheyne. Chelsea's boardroom must have been recklessly deranged. Almost immediately the three Scottish stooges became the focus of an acrimonious dispute about wages, trade unionism and bonus payments. The dispute amounted to a fledgling display of player-power and a dress rehearsal for the Bosman ruling, and the football player's campaign to secure greater freedom of contract.

The Scots argued bitterly with the Chelsea board and as the dispute

unfolded it became increasingly divisive and acrimonious. Jackson was virtually forced out of the game at the age of 26 and never played professionally again, while Cheyne was driven overseas to the French club Nimes.

Only Hughie Gallacher survived. But not for long.

Farewell my lovely

Throughout his days at Chelsea, Gallacher had been contesting a long and painful divorce case with his first wife. He had lost the first action in 1926, failed on appeal and finally won the case in 1934. After years of expensive legal fees, the court revealed that Gallacher had debts of £787, a massive sum for the times, and he was declared bankrupt.

It was at this crisis point in his career that Gallacher, now 32, signed for Derby County. A £200 signing-on fee was paid directly to London's Carey Street Bankruptcy Court.

Hughie Gallacher's career was a microcosm of the kind of scandals that would decorate Scottish football over the next 60 years. Drink, on-field violence, erratic behaviour, public notoriety, breaches of the peace, disputes with management, broken curfews, acrimonious transfers, divorce, headlines, bankruptcy and skirmishes with the law were to become the unofficial milestones which marked Scottish football's ascent into the realm of creative corruption.

Hughie Gallacher's career was a microcosm of the kind of scandals that would decorate Scottish football over the next 60 years

Gallacher and his son, Hughie junior, in 1950

Sadly for Gallacher, the man with the greatest goal scoring ratio that ever played for Scotland, the worst was still to come.

The demon drink

In May 1957, seven years after his wife Hannah had died of a heart attack, Hughie Gallacher hit rock bottom. Drink was an increasingly important and self-deceiving prop in his life. He had long since retired from competitive football and like his tragic contemporary, the boxer Benny Lynch, Gallacher only had memories to live on.

After a domestic fight, his son was taken into care and Hughie was summoned to appear before Gateshead Magistrates Court, charged with child abuse. The day before the case was due to be heard, Gallacher walked towards the railway line near his Gateshead home.

As he passed two small boys on the banking, he brushed against one of them and simply mumbled "Sorry." It was Gallacher's last goodbye.

Driven to the edge of despair and traumatised by the prospect of a court case that deeply injured his pride, he threw himself in front of an express train ironically bound for Scotland.

Hughie Gallacher was killed instantly. The decapitated body of one of Scotland's greatest footballers lay by a railway line near Gateshead in contorted peace. The *Newcastle Journal's* final epithet was a simple but sentimental headline:

"Hughie of the Magic Feet is Dead".

But the legacy he leant us lives on in that bit of Scottish football that refuses to compromise. The greatest injustice in Gallacher's life was that he was born in an era where he could never really profit from his substantial skills, and he grew up at a time before television could immortalise his genius.

To this day the tabloid press must mourn the lost headlines of Hughie Gallacher. ◊

3

BARRY'S WORLD

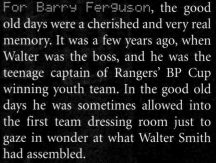

It was 2001. Scottish football was less than halfway through its annual odyssey, and Barry Ferguson had a brainwave. Something had to be done to restore the pride of Scotland's richest club. Rangers had assembled the most expensive team in the history of the game but their wealth was unwinding. By February they were already out of Europe, defeated in the CIS Insurance Cup and trailing rivals Celtic in the quest for the SPL championship. Dick Advocaat's reign as club manager was in crisis. A cold winter wind swept through the hair-pieces of the nation.

In times of adversity a club looks to its captain. This time Rangers' young Scottish skipper was up for the challenge. Barry Ferguson had a brainwave; it was time to revitalise one of Rangers' oldest and dearest traditions. It was time to bring back the bender.

As Ferguson surveyed the Ibrox dressing room he was unimpressed by what he saw. Tore Andre Flo, a lanky Norwegian, had cost the club £12m and was Scotland's most expensive player ever. So far he hadn't kicked a ball. The shirking Italian Marco Negri was still hanging around and over in the corner a French goalie called Lionel something was whingeing about the lavender scent on the dressing room soap. In Barry's world people called Lionel appeared at the London Palladium, not at fortress Ibrox.

Two words sprang to Barry Ferguson's young and untutored Scottish mind. Two words that seemed to encapsulate his team mates flowed effortlessly from Barry's lips. The two words were 'pure' and 'fannies'. None of them would have been able to hack it in the good old days.

For Barry Ferguson, the good old days were a cherished and very real memory. It was a few years ago, when Walter was the boss, and he was the teenage captain of Rangers' BP Cup winning youth team. In the good old days he was sometimes allowed into the first team dressing room just to gaze in wonder at what Walter Smith had assembled.

Surveying the Ibrox dressing room in the bygone days of yore was a different matter. There was 'The Goalie', Andy Goram, with his tombstone teeth and mullet hairdo. There was John Brown, a man whose body would never mould in the grave. There was Durranty and Super Ally, the terrible twins of the dressing room. And there were Fergusons galore. His big brother Derek had moved on, but there was Ian Ferguson; okay he might be teetotal but he hung out with a hard mob in the East End and was always handy in a ruck. And there was 'Drunken'

Duncan Ferguson. The big man was radio rental, the first Scottish footballer to be jailed for assaulting a fellow professional on the pitch. Just a wee head-butt, but he had form so they banged him up. Now *that's* what you call a dressing room.

Then there was always Charlie Miller, ready to go off the rails if he fell in with the wrong crowd. And just to be sure he did, Rangers signed 'Gazza', the most lavishly gifted English footballer of his generation – and a one-man disaster area.

With Celtic 13 points clear in the SPL race, Barry wished the guys were still there. When he got depressed watching Henrik Larsson on *Scotsport*, he would cast his mind back to the dressing room to a place alive with laddish misbehaviour and scurrilous scandal.

There was only one answer to Rangers' plight – they should kick out the fannies and bring back benders. Any team worthy of playing in a Rangers jersey should be able to wreck a pub inside ten minutes, and the last one to Barlinnie is a scabby donkey.

Party animals

On 1 March 2001 the *Daily Record* published a report that Rangers fans feared and prayed for in equal measure. Under the headline "Let's Party Back to the Top", Ferguson claimed the only way to peg back runaway League leaders Celtic was to bring back dressing-room bonding, and spice up the club's good-time image.

The arrival of high-profile foreign imports at Ibrox had profoundly changed the dressing-room culture and there was a widespread suspicion that the Dutch players in particular had brought their infamous divisiveness with them.

According to Ferguson a revitalised dressing room was the answer to Rangers' woes. "You don't have to involve alcohol all the time," he said, hedging his bets, "although there's nothing wrong with having a few drinks, letting your hair down to escape from the pressures of football."

Earlier in the season Ferguson had not quite got the hang of how to escape from the pressures of football. After a high-octane Old Firm match, he went clubbing to a bar in Bothwell, dressed in a Rangers tracksuit. A fight duly erupted after Ferguson told a crowd of local militants that he was entitled to go for a drink in his 'working clothes.'

This was the spirit that Rangers were missing.

Goram the Goalie was the first to back Ferguson. "I don't know which came first – the winning or the trips to the boozer – but it was a magnificent combination." By then on the brink of

> *"I don't know which came first – the winning or the trips to the boozer – but it was magnificent combination"*

Taxi for Ferguson

leaving Motherwell, where he had played for two seasons, Andy Goram's fond memories had never strayed far from Ibrox. "We had something special," he remembered nostalgically. "It was something natural that can't be manufactured. There was a lot made of our nights out and bevvy sessions,

but nobody could fault our effort and commitment on the pitch."

Nor, indeed, their commitment off the field.

Trouble at the dentists

To fully appreciate the lawless camaraderie of the Ibrox dressing room you

have to go back to an era when Barry Ferguson was barely out of primary school.

The 1989–90 season will go down in the history of Scottish football as the year that clubs were rebuilt. Rangers were taken over by the steel magnate David Murray, the club's shares were revalued and a new epoch of 'financial football' gripped Scotland. Rangers Bonds were sold to the fans and in every fiduciary respect the club was restructured.

But when it comes to restructuring clubs, that particular season belonged to Falkirk, then struggling to find consistency in the First Division. Their first team squad toured the country restructuring any club unfortunate enough to let them in. The Metropolis Nightclub in Saltcoats was first to go.

In November, manager Jim Duffy resigned saying: "I have too much respect for football to be involved with players who do nothing but tarnish it and the image of Falkirk." A 24-year-old man suffered facial injuries in the incident and two Falkirk players were reported to the Procurator Fiscal. A few months later the action moved to the Clubhouse Disco in Grangemouth, where another two Falkirk players were cleared of causing a disturbance.

It was always likely that Rangers under their ambitious corporate management would dominate the new League setup. But even the most optimistic Rangers fan could not have predicted how dominant the club would become, or the generation of players that lay ahead.

Official history will mark the arrival of David Murray as the beginning of the Rangers revolution. But Hampden Babylon can trace the real modern roots of the club to a rammy at a nightclub in East Kilbride, and the first time that the tabloid press focused on two players who would span the next ten years of the club's history: Ally

"It's either probation or, at worst, a move to Killie"

"Keep smiling – they think you're Fred MacAuley"

McCoist and Ian Durrant.

Durrant was a player of prodigious talent. In a Rangers team that ranked as the most expensive side in Britain, he was that increasingly rare phenomenon, a local boy made good. Durrant stood out as the genuine article. He was a midfield player with vision, versatility and ambitious temperament, destined to become one of Scotland's best international prospects. But like some of his great predecessors in the Rangers midfield, players like Slim Jim Baxter and Graeme Souness, Ian Durrant was not averse to scandal.

The Scottish tabloid press first discovered Durrant in September 1987 on an ill-fated night out in East Kilbride with two other Rangers players, Ally McCoist and Ted 'Tin-Man' McMinn. Durrant was not directly involved in the incident. In fact, he was cleared of all charges when he appeared at Hamilton Sheriff Court.

But his team mate McCoist, who for the next 20 years was to charm his way out of arrest or serious ill-repute, was fined £150. The crime was punching a local teenager, who had supposedly taunted the Ibrox star when they came out of what was euphemistically described in the press as "a local nightspot".

The court reports of the incident at East Kilbride make fascinating reading. According to the evidence, the Ibrox trio was taunted with shouts of "You're fucking useless" and "Orange bastards". Angered by this outburst on his home soil McCoist, who had briefly been a civil servant in East Kilbride before signing for his first club St Johnstone, allegedly turned on a local tax officer Craig Samson proffering a uniquely Glaswegian greeting – "Do you want a square go?"

The court heard that Ian Durrant took no part in the proceedings. But McCoist punched Samson, knocked his two false teeth out, and according to evidence shouted: "Come here and I'll really give your dentist something to worry about."

Samson claims he ran to the local constabulary for sanctuary and was chased to the door of a nearby police station by McMinn. The court rejected this part of the testimony and Big Ted was free to go. By the time the case had come to court, Durrant had established himself in the Rangers first team and McMinn had been transferred to Seville. Leaving Glasgow with great relief after the trial, McMinn uttered a familiar chorus: "Being a Rangers player you are a target wherever you go."

Run out of town

Within a matter of months, Durrant, a stylish midfielder with a taste for casual designer clothes and side-cropped haircuts, was the biggest target in town. The rising star of the Ibrox firmament had a one-way ticket to notoriety.

On 30 March 1988, a red Renault Turbo drove into Glasgow's Stewart Street police station. Inside the car were 21-year-old Durrant and his solicitor; at the station a squad of CID detectives anxiously waited to quiz him about another disco brawl. In a scene that could have been plundered from a 'B' movie, Durrant later left the station at high speed refusing to comment. A senior police officer simply said: "A man is the subject of a report to the procurator fiscal in regard to incidents that occurred at the premises of Panama Jax disco on the Clyde walkway in Glasgow, in the early hours of March 28."

Subsequently Durrant was dropped from the Rangers first team and in a tabloid story bordering on parody his girlfriend at the time, Jade Oliver, said "I'll Stand By My Rangers Bad Boy". To ensure their readers were given the full context of the Durrant saga, the *Daily Record* helpfully added that Jade was a Lanarkshire hairdresser "with a stunning figure who wants to be a topless model".

Jade's sister Tracy was less lucky in love. In a fearsome foursome, she had drawn the short straw and for several weeks had been dating another member of the Ibrox Firm, the inspired but wayward midfield player Derek Ferguson. Ferguson, McCoist and Durrant's friendship became one of the major talking points of Scottish football as the 1980s drew to a close. They were important members of Graeme Souness's born-again Rangers side, and their future as superstars of Scottish football was virtually secure. But in their young days all three seemed to have a magnetic attraction to trouble and in the case of Durrant a capacity for tragedy that made him as much a victim of football as a star.

Watching their careers gloriously overexposed in the tabloid press was Derek Ferguson's doe-eyed kid brother, a boy by the name of Barry.

The tale of the 'fat cow'

It was a kebab shop on Glasgow's Paisley Road West that featured in the notorious 'Fat Cow' saga, a story of such bizarre misbehaviour it managed to encompass racism, sexism, sectarianism and violence. Step forth Ferguson, Durrant and the carry-out crew.

Durrant and two others admitted that on 4 May 1989 in the Lean Cuisine Carry-Out, they conducted themselves in a disorderly manner, shouted, swore and committed a breach of the peace. Durrant, by then 23 and an emergent Scottish international, was part of a noisy "rabble" accused of insulting one of the Lean Cuisine's other customers, a local woman who was on a night out with several friends including an Iranian

He's blue, he's white, he eats kebabs and fights: Durrant leaves after another court hearing

In a conflict that followed, the court heard that Durrant repeatedly shouted at the woman, calling her a "fat cow"

Boy Wonder, Boyd wonders?

thrown an empty beer glass on to the M8 motorway. Durrant, Ferguson and another man had supposedly rung the taxi from the Horseshoe Bar, possibly the most public of Glasgow's many public houses, and Ferguson emerged from the bar carrying the pint glass.

It was bad press of this kind that led Rangers to lose patience with Ferguson. He had already been fined £2,000 by Graeme Souness after failing to report for training the morning after a reserve team party and missed the 1989 Skol Cup Final against Aberdeen when he injured his shoulder in what the club described as "dressing-room horseplay". It was only a matter of time before he left.

In the midst of his hostile bid to take over Hibs, the controversial Hearts Chairman Wallace Mercer paid £750,000 for the estranged Ferguson whose capacity for trouble and tremendous ball skills made him one of Scotland's most bewildering and infuriatingly gifted players. Derek Ferguson never fully delivered on his immense promise and drifted down the divisions. Before the millennium was out he had been overshadowed by his younger brother and periodically appeared in the press either to offer brotherly advice to Barry or more tragically to talk about his seriously ill child. It remains a mystery and a shame that Derek Ferguson grew up and took on the deep challenges of adulthood when his career was receding.

The injury that denied Rangers the talents of Durrant and marked out a profound watershed in his career took place on 8 October 1988, in one of the worst fouls ever perpetrated in Scottish football. Durrant was badly injured by the Aberdeen player Neil Simpson after a tackle that scarred relationships between Rangers and Aberdeen for the next ten years.

Durrant spent 40 days in hospital

student. In a conflict that followed, the court heard that Durrant repeatedly shouted at the woman, calling her a "fat cow", as others subjected the Iranian to a barrage of racist abuse. As the woman ran to a nearby car they were pursued, the car was kicked, beer was thrown and sectarian songs were chanted. Durrant was fined £200. Ferguson was cleared after the judge

described the evidence against him as "a shambles".

More hot stuff

A few months later Ferguson was in hot water again. A taxi driver reported him to his licensing authority claiming the Rangers player – who at the time was on loan to Dundee – had rolled down the window of a taxi and

> *He implausibly claimed, "It was a case of self-defence. I hit the guy, I had a glass in my hand"*

and hours of painful rehabilitation before the reconstructed leg began to respond. After a six-hour operation on his damaged leg, Durrant awoke to read a newspaper report saying his career was finished. At the time when he most needed a break, his father, a profound influence on his career, died. "To be honest I've cried," said Durrant. Few people would grudge him his tears. Over 10,000 turned up to see Durrant return to Rangers reserve team and within weeks he made the final act of contrition. "Those days are definitely over, I liked a pint but I suffered the consequences in a very big way."

Queer logic

In what must be one of the cruellest ironies of Scottish football, Durrant's off-field behaviour and his horrific injury have a peculiar and tangled logic. His injury took place against a background of unprecedented feuding and violence in Scottish football when the competitive climate of the Premier League had boiled over into animosity. Grudge matches were commonplace, revenge tackles were a weekly occurrence, old scores were settled and professionalism disintegrated into calculated violence and animosity. At its worst, the Scottish

Sectarian fall-out

Celebration never had such a sour taste as it did in May, 1999. Big-spending Rangers had just won the treble with room to spare by beating Celtic in the Scottish Cup final. But while everyone associated with Rangers FC should have been basking in glory, the resignation of Donald Findlay as the club's vice-chairman dragged the club into disrepute.

What should have been a time of glorious self-satisfaction became a nightmare and the fans couldn't celebrate the team's significant achievements without the toxic fall-out of sectarianism. Degraded by bad press, Rangers became hidden champions, a club that could not celebrate their achievements in private without being pursued by shame.

I'm not on Donald Findlay's Christmas card list and unless they find the suffocated bodies beneath my floorboards, I have no plans to draw on his formidable legal skills. So there's nothing much to lose by joining the queue of commentators that castigated Findlay but allow me to do quite the opposite and come to the defence of Donald Findlay Q.C.

> **The fans couldn't celebrate the team's significant achievements without the toxic fall-out of sectarianism**

Let's start from the points we can broadly agree on. Findlay was caught on videotape leading Rangers fans in a medley of sectarian songs, at a private function, after his team had won the Cup. He was not charged with any criminal offence – although he was subsequently fined £3,500 by the Faculty of Advocates after a complaint of professional misconduct – and no complaints were made to the police. The case of Donald Findlay is therefore not a criminal matter; it is a question of taste and judgement.

Findlay's mistake was to act in a manner that is inappropriate to an office-holder of Scotland's biggest club. He brought the club into disrepute not because his actions were uncommon but because the rules of behaviour have changed. Findlay was guilty of associating Rangers with values that have been at the heart of the club for over a hundred years but which are no longer fashionable.

In the past Findlay joked that he has never forgiven his mother for being born on St Patrick's day. I am perplexed that anyone attaches significance to this. What we know of Findlay's biography points to a close relationship with his mother and certainly not a childhood riven with the wrong birthday. His remarks were made in more innocent times – it was a joke with a vengeful aftermath, one he probably regrets cracking.

Nor was it fair to heap significance on Findlay for defending clients accused of sectarian hate-crimes. He is a defence counsellor – that's his job. He defends all sorts of people, from truly hateful characters to innocent people wrongly implicated in crime. Significantly, he has defended very high-profile cases involving Catholic criminals and a measure of his fairness is that rogues of every religious persuasion beat their way to his door.

Like his legal predecessor Nicky Fairbairn, Findlay has a penchant for camp suits, daft ties and arguably even dafter political views but eccentricity alone does not make you a bigot. To lay that charge at Findlay's door would require proof that he discriminates against people because of their religion and there is not a shred of proof to back that argument.

Scotland is too quick to associate tainted culture with bigotry. No-one who regularly attends football matches can be remotely surprised by Findlay's repertoire. When Rangers are the visitors, the same four songs are sung ad-nauseum, and are now so well known they have been virtually drained of their sectarian origins. Findlay's repertoire is now nothing more than a crushing unimaginative bore.

Sadly, for Rangers fans they support a club steeped in heritage but with no credible anthem. In that sense we should look back on Donald Findlay with pity rather than anger. When he stood up in front of the prying eyes of a video camera the night his team won the treble, the only songs that came naturally to his lips were the same weary sectarian dirges that have bored Scottish football rigid over decades.

For a man who prides himself on his flamboyance, it must be a grave personal disappointment to him that his greatest crime was a lack of imagination. So in defence of the likes of Donald Findlay, I would have asked for lenience on the grounds of diminished responsibility, leaving the ladies and gentleman of the jury with the thoughts of opposition fans throughout Scotland and a sentiment that has been chanted at football matches for more years than I care to remember.

'Glasgow Rangers, Glasgow Rangers, Can you sing a football song?'

Spackman supposedly called Goram a "fat bastard". In his own words, The Goalie cracked and belted him twice

League had disintegrated into a skilful equivalent of tribalism. Rangers versus Aberdeen. Hearts versus Motherwell. Durrant versus Simpson. Every game had its angry subtext, every incident had a past, and every team had its reason to seek revenge.

As the Eighties drew to a close, an Aberdeen player Ian Porteous briefly and spectacularly upstaged Durrant and Derek Ferguson's exploits. Porteous was given a free transfer by the club after an incident at Mr G's nightclub in Aberdeen, where he admitted striking Kevin Morrison with a glass, causing him severe injury. The victim was scarred for life and Porteous was fined £1,000 and ordered to pay a further £1,000 compensation to the injured man. In his defence Porteous implausibly claimed, "It was a case of self-defence. I hit the guy, I had a glass in my hand."

Porteous headed for Denmark where he played for FC Herfolge but soon returned to Scotland to sign for Kilmarnock. The Ayrshire club were forced to pay one of the most unusual signing-on fees in the history of football: a cheque for £2,000 to stop an arrest warrant being filed against their new midfielder.

When the Kilmarnock board agreed the exceptional payment, no-one would have dared predict that more than ten years later they would be signing two of Scottish football's most bankable assets. When the sun faded on their Ibrox years, Killie bought the evergreen Durrant, and his ageing sidekick Ally McCoist, who by then was a national legend and a successful TV personality.

To ensure his dressing room was never dull Killie manager Bobby Williamson, previously a player at Ibrox, also chucked in a bonus. He signed a reforming alcoholic and self-confessed drug abuser Andy McLaren. At the age of 15 McLaren had played in Hampden's only ever World Cup final, when Scotland lost on penalties to a heavily bearded Saudi Arabian under-16 team. But that's another story.

Caravan of love

As the 2000–1 season drifted slowly from Rangers' grasp, Barry Ferguson looked on in anguish. Beaten by Dundee United in the cup and Dundee in the league, the most expensive team ever assembled in Scotland would end the season without a sniff at a trophy. Manager Dick Advocaat blamed a horrendous injury crisis and the fans held responsible the bungling Dutchmen, Ricksen and Konterman. Perhaps the only person to escape criticism was the German 'keeper Stefan Klos, but Barry's fantasy Ibrox eleven would never stretch to a German between the sticks. There was a better keeper in the SPL; he was playing at Motherwell now but his heart and soul were at Ibrox. They even called him 'The Goalie'.

Barry's mind drifted back to the time when Andy Goram could start a bender in a synagogue.

When he first arrived in Scotland, a rookie keeper from Oldham with a

Would the owner of the giant willie warmer please remove it?

pronounced Lancashire accent and a love of cricket, there were no outward signs that Goram would become a reckless legend. But no-one has done as much for the cause of soccer scandal as The Goalie.

Goram joined Rangers from Hibs in 1991 and surprisingly identifies Hibs fans as the supporters he dislikes most in Scotland. "As soon as I left to join Rangers, he once said, "I was pilloried." Playing against type, he was the fall-guy in a Skol Cup semi-final when a rare slip up cost Rangers heavily and the Hibees won 1–0. But for the remainder of his Ibrox career Goram rarely played a bad game when it mattered. He saved his best games for Old Firm derbies and famously the Celtic boss Tommy Burns once said that the testimony on his tombstone would read: "Andy Goram broke my heart."

In his ghostwritten biography Goram refreshingly admits to a few dressing room bust-ups over the years. One of the most revealing came after a league match against Aberdeen in 1992, when Goram was beaten by a long-range shot from the Dons mid-fielder Roy Aitken. Goram blamed team mate and former English inter-nationalist Nigel Spackman for not closing Aitken down and carried his complaints back into the dressing at half-time.

In the exchange that followed Spackman supposedly called Goram a "fat bastard". In his own words, The Goalie cracked and belted him twice. According to Goram, Spackman "went down and curled up on the floor like a hedgehog."

The dressing rooms of Scottish foot-ball have not been a happy habitat for people called Nigel. The name seems

to crystallise a kind of effete Englishness that Scots love to mock. But in truth change was seeping through Scotland and Goram did much to stretch the stereotypes. He was born in Lancashire but always felt Scottish. He played cricket, a game that has never captured the popular imagination north of the border, and went on to play for Scotland with the willow bat.

He speaks with an accent that is part-Govan part-Gigglesworth and has a mouth that owes a debt to Stonehenge.

Late night lust
In November 1994 Goram's second wife Tracey Fitzpatrick, a former croupier whom he met in a casino, hit him for a £250,000 divorce settlement. The divorce set the agenda for a decade of what one newspaper

Goram thought it was McCoist winding him up and he told the world's most famous football manager to "piss off"

described as "boozy dust-ups and mounting gambling debts."

The trivial incidents were by far the best. Goram was said to have enjoyed a love romp with a well formed glamour model by the dubious name of Olga Orbs, and in one infamous incident had reportedly enjoyed a session of late night lust in a caravan with a teenage girl. In this particular love tryst it was rumoured that Andy had worn women's knickers, long before David Beckham had rendered them *de rigeur*.

1n 1998 Goram provoked the kind of controversy that anyone outside Scotland or Ireland would struggle to comprehend. At a volatile Old Firm match Goram took the field wearing a black armband. The game was played shortly after the death of the dissident Ulster loyalist Billy 'The Rat' Wright, who had been assassinated in the Maze Prison in Belfast by a group of fellow loyalist inmates.

Goram denied that he was showing sympathy for Wright and that the band was worn as a personal tribute to a great aunt who had died in Lancashire. The fact that the aunt had died months before and that his own mother was sceptical about his excuse did little to support the goalkeeper's theory.

If true, such misdemeanours were part of the Holy Grail of pop journalism in Scotland in the years that Rangers ruled supreme over Scottish football. Graham Roberts was accused of conducting Rangers fans singing 'The Sash', Paul Gascoigne was caught playing an imaginary flute twice in his combustible career, and a few years after, Goram was unknowingly photographed in front of a UVF flag.

With the armband incident still fresh in the mind Goram shocked Scottish football by walking out on the national squad as they prepared for the World Cup Finals in France, and the chance to play in the curtain raiser against defending champions Brazil.

It was a rash and mysterious decision, which Goram has never satisfactorily explained. He was being pursued daily by the tabloid press and was increasingly resentful of intrusions into his private life. Goram was the kind of footballer whose closet housed more skeletons than the Kelvingrove Museum, and the press knew it. But for the majority of fans that was what set him apart from the teetotal fitness fanatics that were gathering in Scottish football. Just when it seemed there was a shop window that would take Andy Goram to the next logical stage of his career – possibly to Italy or Spain – he simply walked away.

No longer an international and fighting a losing battle round the midriff the future looked mediocre. In fact it was worse: Motherwell. Goram joined the rump of glamour players that greeted the millionaire John Boyle's arrival at Fir Park. There was the former Ibrox star John Spencer, Chelsea's Pat Nevin, a winger with a taste for Picasso, Dali and independent rock, and a goalie with a taste for card-schools and creaking caravans.

For once I'm innocent

Just when most people had predicted that Goram's career was coming to an end a remarkable and unprecedented thing happened. Manchester United faced an injury crisis in its bid to retain the Champion's League. The club's first choice keeper, the bald French World Cup winner Fabian Barthez was ruled out. Most of the world's top keepers were contractually tied to other clubs or had already featured in a European tournament; but not Motherwell and not Andy Goram.

Sir Alex Ferguson, who had given Goram the first of his 43 Scotland caps, lifted the phone and offered the hefty 37-year-old keeper a last chance

at greatness. The sinews of the Ibrox dressing room still deep in his body, Goram thought it was Ally McCoist winding him up and he told the world's most famous football manager to "piss off" before realising that Lady Luck had caressed his inside leg one last time.

By a bizarre twist of fate that only Andy Goram's career could accommodate he had actually been in Manchester the week before, returning from a holiday in Italy where he was visiting the former Rangers player Rino Gattuso, by then playing in Serie

Rangers have always been a team fixated with the past. A domineering marble staircase still greets visitors to the club's Ibrox stadium. But the staunch Protestant traditions on which the club was founded are loosening and the iron rod of discipline that ruled over the club when the legendary Bill Struth was boss has all but disappeared. Rangers players were once obliged to wear club blazers at all formal occasions – now the shellsuit will do.

But for Hampden Babylon discipline exists for one reason: to be

"I've done a lot of things in the past and have suffered the consequences but I'm damned if I'm going to take it when I've done nothing wrong"

A with AC Milan. Quite what they discussed on holiday remains a mystery of historic proportion, but the only plausible explanation is Ibrox and the dressing room from hell.

By chance Goram's flight home had been re-routed to Manchester and a gang of drunken holidaymakers had surrounded him. Fearing that the mob would get out of hand on the next leg of the flight, armed police were called, and a sober Andy was prevented from travelling. Fortunately one of the cops was a pal of his Motherwell team mate Greg Strong and the incident was defused.

In an outburst of understandable honesty he admitted that for the first time in his life he was innocent. "I've done a lot of things in the past and have suffered the consequences but I'm damned if I'm going to take it

ritually ignored. Shagging in caravans, fighting with bar stools and getting lifted at Kebab shops. This is the stuff of legend and the collective spirit of one of the greatest teams in the history of Scottish football.

Barry Ferguson looked at the team he was meant to lead and shed a tear for the past – not one of them could be trusted to deck a bouncer. He could only marvel at the genius of the past. Stretching their tender muscles in front of him were the blundering Bert Konterman, an Aussie called Tony Vidmar and a Dutch defender who had been called after an Abba song – Fernando Ricksen. None of them would relish a wet night at Tannadice. You couldn't trust them to deck a bouncer or win a fight with the polis. Pure Fannies. By the way.

Pure fannies. ◊

4

WHAT SHALL WE DO WITH THE DRUNKEN SAILOR?

History has unsteady feet. As Scottish football staggered through the decades not every step forward was sure-footed. In fact, one of the greatest threats to the culture of Scottish football came in the 1990s when a generation of professional footballers turned their backs on one of the country's most esteemed traditions – the bender.

Scottish international John Collins was one such traitor. Curiously for a man who has played for both Celtic and Hibs, Collins believed in the bizarre idea that keeping fit was a matter of principle. He stopped short of uttering the famous abstentionist motto – "my body is a temple" – but nonetheless he was one of a new breed of career athletes whose life revolved around pasta diets, skills training in the afternoon and a deep dialogue with the club physiotherapist. The snooker hall did not feature on the Richter scale of his imagination.

Of course, Scottish football was not always like that. Scotland once led the world in misbehaviour and no history of football would be complete without a hangover.

There is a song in the repertoire of Scottish football fans which reflects unkindly on the character of those gallant heroes who have made untold sacrifices to represent their country in bygone days. The song is usually sung when the fans are possessed with passion and wandering through the streets of some unsuspecting city on the way to a match. It is a story of disrepute:

"We drink beer, we drink wine.
We're the Scotland forward line."

The fact that Scotland fans seek refuge in a debauched image of the team reflects a special relationship between the supporters, their athletic heroes and a magical elixir called bevvy.

Tales of debauchery are legion in Scottish football. Every fan will have their own personal memory – a wild weekend at Wembley, a rammy at the taxi rank, or a unplanned piss-stop where someone fell through a hedge. Sooner or later, as the stories unfold, a Scottish footballer staggers through the story adding a new level of absurdity to the proceedings.

What we should always remember about these folk legends is that some are true, some are false, and most have been embroidered in the interests of pub hilarity. Some have been recounted so often they are part of the apocryphal armada of football. What really happened the night that Jimmy Johnstone set sail on the seven seas?

Wee winger with flash motor

Crime of the ancient mariner

It was a tranquil Spring night on the Ayrshire coast. Local fishermen pulled in their nets, seagulls hovered elegantly overhead, a mild breeze caressed the coast, the ripple of the incoming tide would have made Barbara Cartland swoon. The only noise that could be heard above the gentle contentment of seaside Scotland was the sound of the national team arriving at the Queens Hotel in Largs.

This was no ordinary busload.

Among the merry passengers were a group of Scotland's most adventurous old tars, hell-bent on celebrating a mid-week victory over Wales.

In order to avoid inflicting worry

There is a special relationship between the supporters, their athletic heroes and a magical elixir called bevvy

and pain on the long suffering team manager Willie Ormond, a gang of players bypassed the hotel and headed for the sanctuary of a nearby bar which was owned by a generous Scotland fan called Ross Bowie. The drinking session that followed stretched until 4 am; the players disproving the theory that time and tide wait for no man.

Time no longer seemed to exist and the tide was soon to discover it was on a hiding to nothing.

As the drink flowed, two of the team's most ancient mariners, the captain Billy Bremner and his legendary bosun Denis Law told tales of yore and led their gallant crew in a chorus of merry football shanties. As they finally rose to leave, it became obvious that one of the crew had spliced the main-brace once too often.

Jimmy Johnstone, the outstanding Celtic winger whose mesmerising dribbling skills had earned him the nickname 'Jinky', was busy mesmerising himself. By his own admission, the man who had won a European Cup medal destroying the best defences in Europe was having trouble finding the door.

As the merry band rolled noisily back to the team headquarters along the sea front at Largs, they indulged in what frustrated managers loyally describe as "high spirits" or if the offenders are defenders it is more accurately described as "horseplay". It is a peculiar expression but one that managers are often forced to resort to when players go too far. In this case, the term does a great disservice to horses. In the entire history of equestrians, there is no record of a horse pissing on a park bench and traducing the sexuality of the England international Alan Ball.

Around the world in 80 nips

According to Jimmy Johnstone's forthright biography, the 'horseplay' reached its peak a few yards from the Queen's Hotel when the Leeds and Scotland goalkeeper David Harvey climbed on top of a beach hut and began throwing stones at his team mates. Wilting under a hail of stones and a hefty dose of the hard stuff, Jimmy Johnstone darted for cover and along with Rangers defender Sandy Jardine found himself hiding in the vicinity of a group of rowing boats.

Johnstone was not entirely at fault. "In my drunken stupor I looked at Sandy and mumbled: 'Fancy a wee trip on the water'," he recalled. Jardine agreed, letting Johnstone in the boat first. "I sat patiently waiting for my buddy to join me," Jinky said. "Eventually I shouted 'Sandy are you

"I Wore Sling Backs" claims Lisbon Lion.

By his own admission, the man who had won a European Cup medal destroying the best defences in Europe was having trouble finding the door

in yet?' Before I knew it I was out to sea. Sandy had given the boat a hefty kick before collapsing on the beach in stitches."

As the boat drifted along the Firth of Clyde towards the open sea Johnstone staggered to his feet and sang a rendition of the Rod Stewart song *Sailing*. In the ensuing commotion he lost one of the oars over board. As the oar disappeared into the distance, his last chance of returning to the team's

hotel with dignity drifted away. A desperate rescue mission was launched. The Celtic player Davie Hay and the late Hibernian full-back Erich Schaedler made the first brave attempt, but they chose a defective boat and capsized almost immediately.

As the remaining renegades shouted and cheered from the shore, the noise woke local residents and members of the official party who dutifully called the coastguard. Hay and Schaedler were rescued but Johnstone was on a one-way ticket to Atlantis.

Although Scotland fans remember Jimmy Johnstone as the drunken hero of the Largs boating trip, a passing thought should be spared for a couple of local brothers, John and Tam Halliday, two old men who luckily owned a boat and had a lifetime's knowledge of the maritime area. When the local police realised Johnstone was out of control and heading for danger, they turned to the Halliday brothers for help. The brothers dutifully responded to the mayday request and immediately set out in their 36-foot launch to search for the bevvied buccaneer.

When the Halliday brothers eventually sighted Johnstone, the boat was drifting aimlessly with the tide. Like a scene from Whisky Galore they approached the boat stealthily, initially believing it was a matter of life and death. The two old men, neither of whom were football fans, had no idea how important the cargo was. The oldest brother asked the culprit what the hell he was doing. "I was," said Jinky, "just going out to fish."

By the time Johnstone was helped ashore, the manager Willie Ormond had been alerted and the story had taken the first few faltering steps into football mythology. Denis Law was on hand with a blanket and presented the shivering Johnstone with the commodity he least required: a glass of hot whisky. The next day as breakfast was being served, the team gave the tiny winger a standing ovation, greeting him with a rousing chorus of the old bar-room classic *What Shall We Do With The Drunken Sailor?* A few days later, Scotland played England at Hampden in front of 100,000 fans. The drunken sailors won comfortably and the delirious home support cheered Johnstone's every move. What better way to taunt the Auld Enemy

than to treat them with reckless contempt?

For weeks after the game Scots fans jokingly demanded that the team abandon traditional training methods and prepare for every match with a raging bender. In the years that followed, several players were to take the concept at face value.

Although Johnstone's maritime adventure has entered the folklore of Scottish football, he was never actually

disciplined over the incident. The manager Willie Ormond claimed the players had been given the night off and therefore a breach of discipline had not taken place. After all, being drunk in charge of a rowing boat is no big deal, just part of the everyday rituals of preparing for a big match.

Ormond's compromise exposed another changing phenomenon in Scottish football, a trend that was to gather momentum over the next two

The oldest brother asked the culprit what the hell he was doing. "I was," said Jinky, "just going out to fish"

"Follow me, there's an Agnews behind the away goal"

decades. Player power was on the rise. Johnstone was almost certainly excused because a group of very vocal team mates under the leadership of the Leeds captain and foreman Billy Bremner were exerting a powerful influence over Scottish footballing affairs. It was an influence that probably undermined and eventually curtailed Ormond's period as manager.

If the manager had wanted to take tough disciplinary action against Johnstone another opportunity arose a few days after the drunken sailor saga. On Thursday 23 May 1974, little more than a week after Jinky had set out on his transatlantic crossing, the player was the focus of a controversial legal wrangle when a Sherriff at Airdrie Sheriff Court postponed a trial involving the Celtic winger to allow him to prepare for Scotland's forthcoming World Cup campaign in Germany.

Johnstone and two other Celtic players, Jimmy Quinn and Pat McCluskey, had been charged with assaulting a Paisley man James Cairney outside Casanova's, a Coatbridge nightclub. Johnstone's defence lawyer was none other than Joe Beltrami, a champion of the legal underdog in Scotland and a lawyer who at the time enjoyed a virtual monopoly on Scotland's most controversial court cases. He was the Donald Findlay of his day – without the whiskers, the Edwardian waistcoat and the obligatory flute.

Such were Beltrami's legal skills that he had already secured one postponement of the trial, citing Celtic's European Cup commitments as a *bona-fide* reason. In those days Celtic were a force in European football and a successful run in the tournament was virtually guaranteed. It is a legal manoeuvre that declined in currency by the early 1980s as the words Celtic and Europe decreasingly appeared in the same sentence. In subsequent years

Scottish teams were regularly dismissed from European competition in the early stages, allowing our footballers to be more readily available for midweek court cases. The days of the Jimmy Johnstone ruling are sadly in the past.

The lion sleeps tonight

Johnstone is the mercurial imp of Hampden Babylon. Throughout his career he has captured the magic and the frustration of Scottish football, darting arrogantly down the wing in a surge of skill then retreating into a shell of indifference.

Jinky was James Dean with a ginger hairdo, an Uddingston rebel without a cause. Born in a small council house in Viewpark in 1944, he rose through the ranks of local schools football and almost joined Manchester United as a teenager before Celtic stepped in. Johnstone's size was both his trademark and a source of torment. As a youngster, growing up in the declining Lanarkshire coalfields, he trained at a local Junior ground wearing his father's pit boots, trying to add strength and shape to his diminutive body. Celtic farmed him out to Blantyre Celtic to toughen him up and it was in the killing fields of Blantyre that he won his first honour, a Scottish Junior cap.

Despite the rigours of Junior football and Celtic's body building sessions, Johnstone remained a dwarf

The free-spending Italian club AC Milan were so taken with him that they offered Celtic a fee of £100,000 for his services

Johnstone sticks to the soft stuff

Jinky goes *Dallas*

He was dropped from a game against England for "not being mentally attuned" after he refused to act as a makeshift linesman in a practice match

amongst giants, a midget who spent most of his career infuriating psychopathic defenders with his dribbling style.

Although he will always be compared to the Rangers winger Willie Henderson, a diminutive showman who won the hearts of the other Glasgow, Johnstone had more than impudent skill on his side. His career coincided with the rise of the legendary Celtic side of the late 1960s, which not only won the European Cup in Lisbon in 1967 but also exerted such a dominance in Scottish football that the rest were also-rans.

Johnstone charmed his way through football, showing the kind of tempestuous skill that either wins games or starts fights, and at his height was the most sought after winger in the world. Apparently, the free-spending Italian club AC Milan were so taken with him that they offered Celtic a fee of £100,000 for his services, only to recoil in fear when the club's manager Jock Stein told him they could only rent him for one game for that amount.

Johnstone's professional career ran the gauntlet of scandal from boat trips to benders and back again. Injury and suspensions restricted his international appearances. Although he was one of Scotland's top players for years, his longest run in the national team was only four matches. He was actually dropped from a game against England for "not being mentally attuned" after he refused to act as a makeshift linesman in a practice match.

Johnstone was always more sinned against than sinning. Unlike some of the self-deluding egotists who have played football alongside him, he was a simple and some might say painfully honest man. His playing style belonged to a bygone era when wingers like Gallacher, James and Morton were part of the nostalgic greatness of Scottish football. Jim Baxter maintained to his dying day that Johnstone's display against Leeds United in Celtic's famous European Cup semi-final was one of the most outstanding solo performances in the history of the game.

"What he did to Terry Cooper should be prohibited by Act of Parliament," was Slim Jim's personal homage.

Johnstone's naively gifted style was in many respects complemented by an equal naivety with the press and public. If his fragile skills made him a figure of immense vulnerability on the pitch, then off the pitch, in the press and in the corridors of football power, Jinky was hacked to bits and full-backs were rarely to blame.

Like so many Scots of his social background, Jimmy Johnstone liked a drink. But in the heady tour of parties, testimonials, public houses and charity functions that come with footballing success, many footballers have discovered to their cost that drink can be an obligation more than a pleasure. In the mighty jungle of Celtic's past, 'Wee Jinky' stood tall, but after 1967 the tiniest of the Lisbon Lions spent many mornings sleeping it off.

"Of all the bars ..."

When Johnstone left Celtic to move south to Sheffield United, by his own confession, he had strayed perilously close to alcoholism. "I began to treat Sheffield like one long party," he once said. "Maybe I wasn't disgracing myself on the park, but I was cheating the Sheffield fans and manager Jimmy Sirrell. Sometimes I would go on the wagon for a few days then have a binge. Looking back it was a serious situation, something I wouldn't wish to go through again. I was going to the dogs."

Johnstone's recollections are a candid appraisal of a career on the skids and although drink and football are part of the untamed humour of Scottish society, they are also a major part of the untold pain.

Alcohol abuse in Scotland is its own special problem, and for all their importance as the working-class aristocracy of Scottish society, footballers are more vulnerable to drink than most. Behind the myth of the big drinkers like Hughie Gallacher and Jim Baxter are the people who didn't quite make it to the realm of myth, the lonely bores, the manic depressives, the failed full-backs and the defeated

The pathetic image of one of Scotland's greatest players working outside a bar owned by another is a far cry from the corporate image peddled by today's football missionaries

unfortunates who had to retire early and find a job in the real world.

When a football career ends and reality tackles back, many footballers are attracted like a magnet to the world they know best. For some it's coaching, for others it's journalism and the media but for most it's the fairground of small businesses and professional scams. When it comes to earning a living there is no more enticing environment than a pub.

Jimmy Johnstone's life after football has been a catalogue of defeats and dismal failures. After Celtic he spent periods of time with San Jose Earthquakes and Elgin City, and watched his hair and his money gradually disappear. "Barmen all over the world acquired a fair percentage of my money," Jimmy regrets "And the rest went down the plughole with various business ventures."

The venture that did most damage to Jinky's bank balance was the Double J Bar in Hamilton, a pub designed to cash in on his name, but destined like so many footballer's pubs to become a financial nightmare. The pub suffered from Johnstone's overtly friendly attitude, to genuine misfortune and to the age-old problem of rubber legs and rubber cheques.

Pub life

The footballer's pub is a peculiarly Scottish obsession. Although they undoubtedly exist throughout the world, only Scotland could resort to something quite as sad as turning a pub into a museum of dispirited sport. Every Scottish town has a local pub owned by an ex-footballer, where diehards can drink in the company of their former heroes. Old programmes and framed football strips decorate the walls and grown-up boys gaze in wonder at the past.

Among the many who have owned pubs at one time or another were Willie Johnston who ran The Port Rae Bar in Kirkcaldy, Doug Smith the ex-Dundee United centre-half had The Athletic Bar in Dundee's Hilltown and former Celtic striker Joe McBride whose hoose was The Wee Mill near Shawfield. Danny McGrain had Danny Mac's at Parkhead Cross and Dixie Deans of Celtic ran Carluke's Station Bar. By far the biggest concentration of football boozers is to be found in the square mile that stretches around Hibernian's Easter Road ground where players like Alex Cropley, Jimmy O'Rourke and Peter Marinello have all had bars. Today mein hosts include former Hearts legend John Robertson, serial Hibee Paul

Kane and ex-Celtic player Yogi Hughes.

For some enterprising ex-footballers like Harry Hood or Willie Miller, a pub is a business opportunity to be run to the highest standards. But for others it could be either a modest earner or perhaps a desperate attempt to grab a livelihood from the cinders of football, an industry that in the past never fully protected the talent it exploited.

When Jimmy Johnstone's bar closed, he was forced to take a series of menial jobs as a lorry driver firstly with Lafferty's Construction Company and then a labourer's job with a gas contractor's, where, ironically, he had to dig gas pipelines which ran past Willie Johnston's pub. The pathetic image of one of Scotland's greatest players working outside a bar owned by another is a far cry from the corporate image peddled by today's football missionaries. At Ibrox they sell specially bottled vintage wine and jeroboams of Rangers champagne – drink is supposedly the stuff of success and aspiration, when we all know in Scotland it can be the elixir of failure.

Football is a drama of extremes, and in the case of Jimmy Johnstone he became both the partner and victim of drink.

Seeing the light

Johnstone has confronted his fall from grace with the kind of honest self-awareness that is rare in habitual drinkers. His thoughts border on the day-at-a-time religion of the reformed alcoholic. "Today I can have a drink like the next man without going over the top," he wrote in his self-confessional biography, "I suppose I have learned my lesson the hard way."

But on the terraces of Hampden Babylon Johnstone's lesson will never be fully learnt. Drink and football are linked by such a strong umbilical cord in Scottish culture that it is virtually

"Denis Law? He couldn't lace our drinks"

Football is a drama of extremes, and in the case of Jimmy Johnstone he became both the partner and victim of drink

impossible to talk about one without the other encroaching. Even the jokes drip with alcohol!

Have you heard the one about the two Scottish footballers who were condemned to death in Panama? They are forced to face a firing squad in the prison courtyard and, predictably, one is sober and the other is steaming. The prison governor tells them they are about to be shot and offers them the choice of dying like men or wearing blindfolds. The drunken winger goes

berserk and tells him to stick his blindfold sideways up his arse. Fearing that the outburst might make their predicament worse, the sober team mate recoils with fear and says "Calm doon wee man. You'll get us intae trouble with the SFA."

Jimmy Johnstone was that winger. ◊

5

DOCTOR STRANGELOVE AND THE LORDS OF DISCIPLINE

No matter where the word 'biscuit tin' is mentioned, it immediately brings to mind Glasgow Celtic, long-famed for its institutional meanness. So when the International Investment Company (ENIC) took control of Tottenham Hotspur in the early months of 2001, they were shocked to find that club too was in possession of a biscuit tin stuffed with cash.

The era of corporate football was tightening its grip on the boardrooms of the English Premier League and Tottenham's new own-

ers were more accustomed to offshore accounts and investment trusts. Surely the biscuit-tin mentality was from a long distant past?

Four days earlier Spurs had dismissed their manager, George Graham, a former Scottish international who had famously managed Tottenham's north London rivals Arsenal. The suspicious tin of cash sent the new owners into a panic. Accustomed to streamlined accounts systems and bank transfers, to stumble on the residue of football's hard cash economy was a wake-up call.

Graham immediately claimed that the club's new owners were trying to smear his name and that the money was nothing more sinister than a cash pile of fines he had taken from players who had strayed from the path of righteousness. Graham also resorted to one of football's favourite clarifications – the money was collected for charity.

Ironically one of the players who was on the receiving end of George Graham's charity tin was the Swiss international Ramon Vega who had been sold to Celtic a few months earlier. Vega painted a picture of almost Victorian discipline in which any breach of predefined codes was punishable by an instant cash fine. "If you were late it was always taken off you as cash," he told the *Daily Mirror*. "Stewart Houston, the assistant coach, would come and say 'You are late, pay a fine.' If it was something bad it would be a big fine."

Stewart Houston and George Graham, who was nicknamed 'The Stroller' because of his languorous style, had played together at Manchester United in the Seventies. Quite simply they had learnt the game in a different era, where rusting turnstiles and the cash economy were simple and effective truths. A manager's job was to instil discipline in reluc-

Football's fatal attraction

tant footballers and if they couldn't break down a wayward spirit they had two options: a humiliating month in the reserves or straight onto the transfer list.

One of the inherent tragedies of George Graham's decline at Tottenham was that he was managing a new generation of players represented by agents and sports brand ambassadors. They were happy to play for different clubs every two years, and always put their own personal welfare above the older values of team effort, playing for the jersey or running off an injury.

It was not that George Graham was out of his time. On the contrary, he was a smart and suave operator. He wore elegant Crombie coats, had the chiselled good looks of an ageing matinee idol and he was a good manager. But

the values that Graham and his generation had aggregated across a career that began in the raw tin-shacked dressing rooms of his native Bargeddie were not easily compromised when football became corporate.

Although the flow of big name players heading south to England had dried up by the Nineties, the upper echelons of Scottish football still valued the lords of discipline that came down from Scotland to exact Presbyterian power over the waifs and strays of the dressing room. The image of a hoarse Scottish disciplinarian barking orders in a tracksuit still had currency. Matt Busby, Jock Stein and Bill Shankly were long dead but their legacy had been handed down to others and by 2001 England's Premiership had almost as many Scottish managers as there were play-

ers. The greatest of them all, Sir Alex Ferguson, had announced his retirement but still had a vice-like grip on Manchester United. George Graham – despite his implication in what the tabloids called 'football bungs' – was still an immensely talented boss who managed Arsenal, Leeds and Spurs. The grumpy Hearts boss Jim Jefferies had been lured south to try to rescue struggling Bradford. Gordon Strachan was a tracksuit boss at Coventry City. Davie Moyes was at Preston, Jocky Scott was at Notts County, while the former Dundee United talisman Paul Sturrock had put health scares behind him to manage the Pilgrims of Plymouth Argyle.

Graham's departure from Tottenham derailed 'The Stroller's' managerial career and it cast a longer shadow over one of football's ingrained traditions – hard case Scottish managers.

By 2001 the Professional Football Association had agreed a strict code for players' fines: money had to be deducted with consent from a player's gross salary and the Inland Revenue informed. The days of instant fines and pre-match bollockings were fading, and the threat of extinction hung over the heads of Scots disciplinarians.

As Scottish managers fought relegation and remonstrated with wayward stars, one man kept a cynical eye on their progress. The uncrowned king of the after-dinner speaking circuit was a retired Scottish manager whose explosive career had set the benchmark by which managerial scandal would be measured. He was known simply as 'The Doc'.

Born to be wild
Thomas Henderson Docherty was born in 1928 in Glasgow's notorious Gorbals, the son of a steelworker and a Glasgow Corporation lamplighter. At the age of eight his father died, by

"What do you mean there's a boundary charge?"

which time the family had moved to The Bowery, an area in the Shettleston district of Glasgow's East End. It was the archetypal hard man upbringing, a tale of single-ends, the Social and supporting Celtic. In his infant years he slept with his mother and two sisters in a single bed – a plank of wood jutting out of the wall.

Docherty was born to be wild. Raised in some of the toughest and most deprived areas of Glasgow, he was a gifted schoolboy footballer with a precocious ability to use poverty to his advantage. From his first sip of welfare orange juice, he was cut out to be a professional Glaswegian. But none of the boys who played with him at St Mark's Roman Catholic Primary School in Shettleston could ever have

"I've been punished for falling in love. This is the most shattering experience in my footballing life"

guessed they were in the company of a very special talent. The world was to christen him 'The Doc' but those who followed his bewildering career as it lurched from one club to another would always know him as Dr Strangelove, a man with a healthy appetite for the physiotherapist's wife.

Scandal has permeated Docherty's career. His most infamous moment came in July 1977 when he was sacked from the manager's post at Manchester United after disclosing the fact that he was having an affair with Mary Brown, wife of the club's physiotherapist, Laurie Brown. In what remains one of the most touching and compassionate statements of his flamboyant career, The Doc told waiting newsmen, "I've been punished for falling in love. This is the most shattering experience in my footballing life."

The idea that The Doc – one of football's dressing-room disciplinarians – could be capable of an emotion as fragile and complex as love, struck his players at Manchester United as one of the great paradoxes of all time. Surely the love-struck Lothario was not the same Doc who bullied them to a successful FA Cup Final? Surely it was not the same Glasgow hard-man that had described football management as jungle warfare? "Lots of managers have to be cheats and con-men," he once told a Football Writers' Association dinner. "People say we tell lies. Of course we tell lies. We are the biggest hypocrites. We cheat. In our business the morals are different. The only way to survive is by cheating. That's the law of our life."

The law of Docherty's life has taken him on a rollercoaster through football management. He had 17 management jobs in total including Scotland, Chelsea, Manchester United, FC Porto and Queens Park Rangers, and he will be immortalised by his own self-deprecating one-liner, "I've had more clubs than Jack Nicklaus, but he used them better."

The gift of comedy

Docherty's greatest gift is his comic resilience. When he was sacked from the manager's job at Preston in 1981 he immediately told the press. "They offered me a handshake of £10,000 to settle amicably. I told them they would have to be more amicable than that."

Docherty's prodigious talent flowered in the late Forties during his National Service. In an attempt to solve the Arab–Israeli crisis, the Highland Light Infantry sent Docherty to Palestine, where he played football for the British Army XI. As Docherty covered every inch of the Palestinian pitches, he was spotted by

"People say we tell lies. Of course we tell lies. We are the biggest hypocrites. We cheat. In our business the morals are different. The only way to survive is by cheating"

"Did you have to wear those socks?"

Walter Waddell, brother of the famous Rangers star Willie Waddell, and on the day of his demobilisation he signed for Celtic. The club paid him the princely sum of £8.

After playing only a handful of games for Celtic, Docherty moved south to Preston North End, where he made his debut on Christmas Day 1949, eventually displacing his mentor Bill Shankly and rising through the ranks to captain the Preston side. Shankly progressed to Liverpool where his disciplinarian approach was tempered by a socialist sophistry, a balance that gained him unique respect in football as he guided Liverpool to an era of unrivalled success at home and abroad.

Docherty's thoughts on football management diverted from Shankly's in one crucial respect: scandal. If FIFA ever had the foresight to forego football and organise the World Cup for Misbehaviour, Scotland would undoubtedly be the bookies' favourite and Thomas Henderson Docherty would be an inevitable choice as manager.

In the mid-1970s, while he was still manager of Manchester United, The Doc frequently appeared on ITV in a commercial for Gillette 2 razor blades. His catch line was, "I can honestly say it's the closest shave I've ever had." Of course it was a complete lie. Nobody has brushed with the law quite like The Doc.

In October 1967, when he was manager of Chelsea, the English FA suspended him for 28 days, for alleged misconduct during a friendly match in Bermuda, where Docherty persistently swore at a black referee. It was a strange misdemeanour but it launched The Doc on a career of unparalleled misbehaviour, which included regular confrontations with the football authorities and inevitable conflict with the law.

By his own admission The Doc is a lawyer's dream come true. In one of those disarming quotes that make him both loathsome and likeable, he once said, "I've been in more courts than Bjorn Borg." For once in his life he wasn't exaggerating.

At the time of his controversial dismissal from Manchester United, the *News Of The World* revealed that a

During his days as manager of Derby County he once told a player "You've got deceptive pace son – you're even slower than you look"

team of private detectives, hired by a group of businessmen closely linked to some of the club's directors, had been pursuing The Doc for nearly two years.

None of the allegations were ever substantiated and in that respect Docherty was the victim of an over-zealous media campaign against him. However, a series of related allegations eventually led to a High Court libel action involving Docherty and two of Manchester United's most prominent Scots players, Denis Law and Willie Morgan.

Gunfight at the Trafford corral

The Morgan affair cuts to the heart of Docherty's character. It was a bizarre incident, which created a vicious and public rift between some of Scotland's most gifted players, and ended up in the ignominy of a High Court hearing. The trouble began in November 1978 when Docherty attempted to sue the Scottish international winger

Willie Morgan over remarks the player made about his style of management on a Granada TV sports programme called *Kick Off*.

Docherty claims he was "written off" by Morgan who described him as "about the worst manager there has ever been." Although the case collapsed and Docherty admitted telling "a pack of lies" in court, it opened up damaging wounds within Manchester United, and created a climate of fear and loathing among leading players that stretches to the present day.

The Manchester United half-back Pat Crerand who had grown up with Docherty in Glasgow painted a picture of extraordinary conflict within the club. "Doc was a bully with the players, he treated them like dirt," claimed Crerand adding that several players disliked him so much they threatened to 'do' him.

Although he had an unrivalled ability to motivate players, Docherty's approach often bordered on theatre of cruelty. He revelled in his ability to inspire players either by encouragement or ridicule. In his autobiography he dismissed Gerry Daly as a player "who lacked grey matter" and during his days as manager of Derby County he once told a player "You've got deceptive pace son – you're even slower than you look."

The image of bullying boss is confirmed by the Willie Morgan affair.

Ironically, Morgan admired Docherty when they first met during the 'mini-World Cup' in Brazil in 1972. He remembers him as a "breath of fresh air" as a manager who single-handedly rejuvenated the Scottish team with his incredible ability to motivate players. When their paths crossed years later at Manchester United, Morgan admits that he "thought the world of The Doc" but

slowly, bit by bit, it began to emerge that Docherty was mistreating some players and scheming against others.

Docherty had been employed to revitalise Manchester United's fading greatness. In his own words he intended to "cut the cancer" out of the Old Trafford dressing room. Sadly one of Docherty's highest profile problems with the club's senior stars was Scotland's Denis Law. He was freed in 1973 and crossed the divide to join

Manchester City but his departure was acrimonious and sowed the seeds of lasting animosity between the two Scots. Ironically Law, implausibly wearing the sky blue of City, scored the goal that eventually relegated Docherty and his United team. Law walked off the pitch, refused to celebrate his goal and never played professional football again. According to popular myth, Law discovered he was on the list to leave Old Trafford from a TV report when he was visiting his sick mother in Aberdeen. The disputes that followed were to drive a wedge between Law and Docherty, and persist with increasing bile and acrimony to the present day. In 1979, when the United team was travelling home from a game in the south, Docherty was attacked by a gang of

"There could only be one winner, and that would be The Doc. He could start an argument in an empty house"

Docherty's Cup runneth over

City fans. He was hospitalised and needed 28 stitches to a leg wound. Denis Law was reportedly on board the train but kept a careful distance from the fight.

Although Law will no longer be drawn on his relationships with Docherty, Crerand and Morgan are forthright in their opinions. Crerand bitterly resents Docherty, who dismissed him as Manchester United's assistant manager and according to the ex-Celtic halfback, the late Jock Stein described Docherty as "nothing but a Glasgow corner boy." Crerand's withering comment was simply, "I didn't think he was even that good."

It is not a description Docherty takes lying down. He once said, "Appointing Crerand was the second biggest mistake of my life." Subsequently, he claimed that the ex-Celt tried to pick a fight with him in the toilets at a function after Manchester United's unsuccessful FA Cup Final against Southampton in 1976 and has dismissed Crerand as a player who had a jealous envy of greater talents.

Throwing punches in an empty house

But undoubtedly, it is the former United and Burnley player Willie Morgan who has most reason to distrust and dislike Docherty. Bitterness set into their relationship after a mid-week international, when Morgan returned to Manchester from Hampden to find that the *Daily Mail* had run a sensational story about a behind-the-scenes bust up between Morgan and his boss. According to Morgan, when he challenged Docherty, The Doc denied being the source of the story and went through the deceptive rituals of ringing the journalist to complain. Then when it appeared the problem had been solved, Morgan alleged he hid outside Docherty's and overheard him ringing

"Just call me Sir Alex"

the journalist again to apologise for his outburst, claiming it was only done to fool the player.

The animosity that set in between Morgan and Docherty and the disrespect it cultivated at Old Trafford is in marked contrast to the towering respect that United fans have for

another Scots disciplinarian, Sir Alex Ferguson.

Born and raised in Govan's Harmony Row, Fergie matched Docherty's working class upbringing, but his early years as an apprentice in the shipyards brought him closer to industrial socialism than the swagger-

The animosity towards Docherty resurfaced years later… when a clearly drunk George Best outlined his reasons for leaving Old Trafford. In a slurred voice he blamed Docherty calling him "a liar and a bullshitter"

ing corner-boy style that Docherty perfected. After a mediocre football career at St Johnstone, Dunfermline and Rangers, Fergie made his real impact in management first at lowly East Stirling then St Mirren, before turning Aberdeen into one of the most respected clubs in Europe. It was all a dress rehearsal for greatness and despite a barren period when he first joined Manchester United, in which he faced the sack and only barely held on to his job, Ferguson became a colossal figure in modern football. He steered United through its most successful era, winning the Champions League and all but turning English football into a one-horse race.

Despite their Glasgow working class origins it would be difficult to find two managers who contrasted the disciplinarian style as profoundly as Docherty and Ferguson. One was callous and driven by the art of the dressing room put-down, the other was skilled in the evasive art of man management, always searching for the hidden dynamic that could turn a player's confidence full circle.

The Morgan affair would not have been allowed to contaminate Ferguson's Manchester United. It had a truly corrosive effect on the club and team morale. A former Manchester

United player, the Northern Ireland international Jimmy Nicholl, who later managed Raith Rovers on an intoxicating UEFA Cup campaign, believes it was all founded on professional jealousy. He believes Docherty perceived Morgan to be a threat to his power base, and was the kind of flamboyant player who had the raw potential to rise to the status that George Best had enjoyed in Docherty's early years at Old Trafford.

"There could only be one winner, and that would be The Doc," Nicholl said. "He is the kind of person who thrives on arguments. He could start an argument in an empty house."

Arguments were a daily occurrence at Old Trafford. Willie Morgan was taken to court and had to terminate a lucrative six-year contract after only nine months. He feels bitterness and betrayal to this day. "Docherty tried to ruin me, my career, and my family. I hate him." The animosity towards Docherty resurfaced years later on a memorable episode of the BBC chat show *Wogan*, when a clearly drunk George Best outlined his reasons for leaving Old Trafford. In a slurred voice he blamed Docherty calling him "a liar and a bullshitter".

Sir Alex Ferguson has had his detractors and there are fans of

opposing clubs who have reason to dislike him. But it would be inconceivable for a player like Roy Keane or David Beckham to turn on their boss with such an animosity, or to dispute his skill so viciously in public. It is equally unthinkable that Manchester United would want to terminate his contract. On the contrary, the club spent the best part of two years trying to delay Ferguson's retirement and finally offered him a lifetime sinecure with the club.

But for all the hatred that has been heaped on Docherty by former players, it was the opposite emotion that attracted Mary Brown to The Doc. When they met she was happily married to her first husband Laurie Brown, a member of Manchester United's back-room staff, and the man who had the questionable job of keeping George Best's body at the peak of fitness.

Docherty was betrothed to his first wife Agnes, an unpretentious Glaswegian whom he had met in the late Forties at a social club dance when The Doc was an aspiring player with Celtic. Agnes and Tommy Docherty's marriage was in many respects typical of their generation and typical of their Catholic upbringing in the west of Scotland. With four children and a stable lifestyle, the break-up of the Docherty's marriage came as a devastating blow to those closest to him. His children have never fully forgiven him and the scandal has scarred everyone involved in The Doc's love life.

The affair happened at the most inopportune moment. Docherty was on the verge of signing a new contract with United, who had just won the FA Cup, and in an act of either remarkable honesty or unmitigated stupidity, he decided to inform the board that he was romantically involved with the physiotherapist's wife.

At first the club treated it as a private

"There are lots of priests at Manchester United," he said at the time, "and some of them are on the board"

Are you dancin'? Are you askin?

matter and The Doc shook hands on a new four-year contract. But within a few hours the mood changed and what Docherty now describes as "unforeseen forces" began to operate. He was summarily dismissed from his job and the scandal broke on the front pages of Britain's national press.

The moral crusade

Undoubtedly Docherty's Catholicism contributed to his downfall. His brother-in-law Stewart Milne, who is married to The Doc's young sister Margaret, maintains that the prevailing Catholic legacy at Old Trafford conspired against The Doc. "There are lots of priests at Manchester United,"

he said at the time, "and some of them are on the board." They wanted to protect the public morality of the club, and wanted Docherty out. Like the Celtic team of his childhood, Manchester United's Catholic heritage ultimately strangled Docherty's faith in the Holy Scriptures and to a lesser extent in that more endearing religion called football.

If Docherty's dismissal from the manager's job at Manchester United had unspoken religious undertones, it had its greatest impact on a close-knit Catholic family back home in Glasgow. Margaret Docherty believes the marriage break-up had a devastating effect on The Doc's ageing mother.

She was nearly 80 years old at the time and had been a devoted parent and strict Catholic all her life. Part of her annoyance was brought about by the fact that she had never met nor heard of Mary Brown, but part of it was fuelled by the fact that her son had broken with the faith. On hearing the news, The Doc's mother broke down in tears. To comfort her a friend said "These days it can happen to anyone." Mrs Georgina Docherty, Mother Glasgow to the end, said, "He is not anyone. He is Tommy Docherty."

It would be unfair to Docherty and his family to end there. At the time of the scandal, many people dismissed the affair as a rash mistake, which would never last. Margaret Docherty describes Mary as being "like a schoolteacher and very proper" – the most unlikely woman that a smart-ass street kid from Shettleston would ever marry. But love and scandal move in mysterious ways. Although 18 years separate the couple, they are happily married and live in Derbyshire with their two daughters Grace and Lucy. As a divorcee, Docherty can no longer take communion and has distanced himself from the Catholic faith, an institution he believes deserted him in his hour of need. He no longer attends the church. But if the Vatican believes it has banished The Doc, the Pope should think again.

Incorrigible to the last, the high priest of scandal has even turned his worst moment into a punchline. In 1987, he walked into the dressing room at non-league Altrincham and turned to the club's physiotherapist Jeff Warburton. With a smile on his face, The Doc turned years of anguish on its head. "How's the wife?" he joked, and walked out the door.

For all his imperious achievements, Sir Alex Ferguson has never cracked a joke as fully formed as that. ◊

6

DON'T SHOOT I'M THE GOALKEEPER

Disasters are part of the tragic landscape of history. Volcanoes, earthquakes, landslides, explosions and raging infernos have engulfed whole communities leaving a trail of death and destruction in their wake.

But Scotland has never had much time for earthquakes: the national football team has secured its own unique monopoly on disasters.

By a farcical inversion of football's heightened history, Scotland has turned its back on triumph and charts its history by disaster and despair. The most memorable episodes in Scottish football are carved into the psyche of Scotland fans like a scar. Let the Brazilians worry about magic; we have calamity on our side.

And when disaster strikes, the people of Scotland are quick to shed their mask of tolerance and the search is on for a scapegoat. Over the last 30 years, when names like Pele, Eusebio, Cruyff,

Müller and Maradona were igniting world football, the people of Scotland could retaliate with their own itinerary of hapless dupes and national scapegoats.

Some have been managers: Andy Beattie, Bobby Brown and the tragi-comic Ally McLeod. Even now decades later, it is virtually impossible to erase the memory of his haunted face sitting in a dug-out in Argentina as the greatest team in the history of Scottish football self-destructed.

But when it comes to scapegoats most have been members of that lonely fraternity of misfits they call goalkeepers. When the firing squad finally arrives, six men in blindfolds will be strung out along the prison wall: Freddie Martin, Frank Haffey, Stewart Kennedy, Jim Blyth, Alan Rough and Jim Leighton.

Gentlemen, you have one final wish.

On 12 June 1990, the morning

after Scotland had lost to an unfancied Costa Rica side in their critical opening match in the Italia '90 World Cup, the *Daily Record* led with an agonising front-page story. It wallowed in alliteration and dredged through the dire, dismal and deplorable depths of defeat. The headline simply said, "Stop the World We Want To Get Off". It was the perfect epitaph for a nation accustomed to World Cup disasters and finely attuned to an endless chorus-line of infamous goalkeepers.

Scotland's capacity for World Cup disaster began in earnest in 1954. In the qualifying stages they were drawn against Finland and Norway and staggered unconvincingly towards the finals, after only 13 members of the pool turned up for a training session at Ayr before the vital away match in Oslo.

"I'll take the rap," said Harry Swan the SFA President, "I got the dates wrong." This simple, naive and incom-

Handball, ref?

prehensible blunder established Scotland's reputation as the team most likely to screw up when it came to a big match preparation. The image died hard. Over 30 years later, when Scotland played in an infamous game in Estonia where the hosts failed to show, there was a stuttering anxiety among the travelling support that maybe we had blown it and turned up at the wrong ground. The game kicked off. John Collins lifted his hands in triumph and the most surreal game in Scotland's history was over. Surreal is the operative word.

The 1954 finals could have been painted by Salvador Dali such was its tortured logic. An SFA selection committee had made the odd decision to pick the team months before the finals, and conspired to select a pool of only 13 players, which barely reflected the best talent available. In fact, the team was chosen so far ahead that the

monumental Rangers defender George Young was omitted because of an injury that cleared up weeks before the team left Scotland. Nonetheless, the unlucky 13 – including two goalkeepers but no obvious captain – departed for Switzerland under the tutelage of manager Andy Beattie.

The 1954 World Cup team will go down in history as one of the most disastrous and ill-prepared rabbles that has ever represented the country abroad. In the opening game of the tournament against Austria, Scotland had forgotten to bring a pennant to exchange with their opponents. It was not the only oversight. The Celtic player Neil Mochan claimed that the 1954 squad was nicknamed 'The Liquorice Allsorts'. According to legend, the SFA had forgotten to provide training strips and the team were forced to wear a multi-coloured melange of club strips and borrowed

jerseys. The blue of Rangers, the green of Celtic, the tangerine of Blackpool and the yellow and red of Partick Thistle clashed in a blinding flash of psychedelia. Scotland had inadvertently invented Acid House. But it was several years yet before the ecstasy of drugs would join their repertory of World Cup disasters.

The 1954 campaign ended in ignominy. Disillusioned with managing the national team, Beattie chose the most inappropriate moment to tender his resignation. He announced his departure just before the kick-off and so Scotland's ramshackle team went out to face the world champions Uruguay stripped of all confidence and tactical direction. They were thrashed 7–0.

The goalkeeper on that fateful day was Freddie Martin of Aberdeen, a talented but unfortunate keeper who let in another seven goals the following year against England at Wembley. Misfortune between the posts apart, Martin was lucky in one crucial respect. At the time, very few Scottish homes could afford television sets so the nation could not witness his performance and judgement was withheld. History and the action replay would be less kind to Scottish keepers in the years to come. By the '70s, when Freddie Martin was playing for a whisky company's office team in Perth, his successors between the sticks were being subjected to intense TV scrutiny.

100 years of solitude
Disaster and dismal performances are part of the bungled heritage of Scottish football. In a country that invests so much energy and passion in the game, the frustrations that defeat and incompetence arouse inevitably breed resentment. In 1954, the accusatory finger of fate pointed at Fred Martin and his manager Andy Beattie,

a relatively successful club manager with seven English league clubs including Huddersfield and Nottingham Forest.

Nearly 25 years later, agitated by the fake euphoria of Argentina, the finger once again turned on a manager and his hapless keeper.

The 1978 World Cup campaign in Argentina will go down in history as the absolute nadir of Scottish football. The myths it unleashed could fill a book. Fist fights shamed the team's base camp at Dunblane Hydro. A bender took place in Perth and two players were caught pissing up a close next to the town's Shanghai Takeaway. A euphoric send-off at Hampden Park sent the nation into a collective frenzy. Then there was defeat against Peru, a disgraceful match with Iran, a drug scandal and then as if victory could be grabbed from the jaws of disaster came a piece of eleventh-hour magic.

Archie Gemmill scored that goal against Holland, the goal that Irvine Welsh's *Trainspotting* accurately described as better than sex. The fact is that despite the weeks of unfolding farce Scotland came within minutes of overwhelming the beaten finalists Holland. All this was part of the real or imagined story of Argentina.

By the last week of May 1978, Scotland was at fever pitch. England had failed to qualify for the finals, Scotland had defeated Wales in an emotional match at Liverpool's Anfield Stadium and Ally McLeod, a supremely patriotic manager given to hyperbole and heart-wrenching nationalism had amassed one of the finest football sides for years. Among the many outstanding players in the Scotland squad were the toothless warrior Joe Jordan, the mercurial Kenny Dalglish and the effervescent Willie Johnston. And an over-abundance of creative midfield players that subsequent Scotland squads could

only dream of, including Don Masson, Bruce Rioch, Asa Hartford, Archie Gemmill, John Robertson and Lou Macari.

The first signs of rust came on the day an early battalion of the tartan army arrived in Cordoba. The *Daily Record* revealed that an acrimonious dispute over cigarette sponsorship was splitting public opinion back home. Money was to become an increasingly divisive issue throughout the campaign and it all began with a packet of fags. Despite protests from the anti-smoking group ASH and in spite of the advice of Scotland's highly vocal health lobby, the team, the manager and the SFA accepted a share of £2 million sports sponsorship from the British American Tobacco Company. The Scottish Health Education Unit counselled the team to withdraw from the deal.

But in a reply that summed up Ally McLeod's capacity for humorous catastrophe the manager responded by saying, "I told him several of our players smoke and it would be untruthful to back an anti-smoking campaign." If McLeod's twisted logic were taken to its conclusion, events over the next two weeks would

"It's the bank for me!"

demonstrate that some members of the Scottish team were ideally suited to sponsoring the work of Alcoholics Anonymous and the Drumchapel Drug Dependency Clinic.

By the time the Scotland team had arrived at the Sierras hotel in Alta Gracia, the rot had set in. The bonus deal the SFA had offered the team to win the World Cup did not match the players' expectations. Behind the scenes squabbles broke out. McLeod, a man not generally regarded as one of life's diplomats, was left to dampen the flames and Scotland's preparation inevitably suffered. On the first night, three members of the squad, the goalkeeper Alan Rough and the Rangers pair Derek Johnstone and Sandy Jardine, left the camp to visit a local casino.

"There was no question of them gambling," McLeod insisted, before adding his own inimitable proof. "They did not have Argentinian money." On their return to the hotel, the three were caught climbing a security fence by armed guards who mis-

His blond perm breezing in the hot night air, he shouted, "Don't shoot I'm the goalkeeper"

took them for Scotland fans. According to legend, Rough told the guards to put their guns away shouting out what has become an apocryphal line in the history of the game.

His blond perm breezing in the hot night air, he shouted, "Don't shoot I'm the goalkeeper."

It was a remark he should have reserved for an ageing Peruvian marksman called Cubillas.

Scotland collapsed in their opening game, losing 3–1 to Peru. The defeat opened the sluice gates and venom flowed through in raging torrents. Drunk? Unfit? Simply crap? Every accusation was thrown at the team; even Tunisia got in on the act. The Tunisian national team had the questionable pleasure of sharing a training camp with Scotland, their manager Abdelmajid Chetali claimed that Scottish players spent most of their time shirking training. "They smoke and drink a lot – especially whisky," he said, trying to reconcile his Muslim abstention with the profligacy of Scots on the rocks.

When it seemed impossible to sink any lower, the team rose to the challenge and sputtered their way through a pitiful draw with Iran, in which an own goal saved them from defeat. "Shamed. Humiliated. And shown up to be fourth rate in front of the world," screamed the *Record*.

Like a row of cascading dominoes, scandal followed scandal. Willie Johnston was sent home for taking drugs, Chrysler withdrew an advertising campaign which showed Scotland supporting the Avenger Saloon, Rod Stewart's *Ole Ola* plummeted down the charts, then finally Scotland got something right. In their final game they defied normal logic and won the hardest game in their section by defeating the much fancied Holland, courtesy of a piece of outstanding arrogance by the diminutive Archie Gemmill. Triumphing against all odds and losing when it seems easier to win is one of Scotland's most endearing faults.

Alone again naturally

Although Gemmill's goal was voted the best in the tournament, the sight of a mesmerised Alan Rough watching in disbelief as a Peruvian free kick flew past him into the net will remain one of Argentina's bleakest moments. The goalkeeper's agony is a specifically Scottish condition. If Franz Kafka was to rewrite *The Trial* and set it in Hampden Babylon, the alienated victim would be a goalkeeper, a solitary figure trapped between the posts, perpetually fearing the penalty. His name would immediately conjure a mood of lonely alienation. The name might be Jim Leighton, Jim Blyth or Stewart Kennedy. But if Kafka was really laying on the angst, he would choose a name

The inevitable World Cup headline

synonymous with pain and defeat. A name like Frank Haffey.

What's the score?

The first month of 1961 witnessed profound activity throughout the world. Yuri Gagarin orbited the earth in the first manned satellite, Stalin's body was unceremoniously removed from the Moscow Mausoleum, counter-revolutionaries attempted to overthrow the Castro regime in Cuba and Scotland were drubbed 9–3 at Wembley.

The goalkeeper that fateful Saturday afternoon in April 1961 was Frank Haffey, who to this day remains the most unfortunate victim of Scotland's greatest football disaster.

Haffey was part of Scotland's erratic tradition, a keeper capable of inspired performances and indescribable blunders, who had edged his way into an unconvincing Celtic team in the early '60s. Frank was never Scotland's first choice keeper; instead that position was held with secure dignity by the Dundee and Tottenham Hotspur keeper Bill Brown, a player who generally defied the image of incompetent Scottish goalkeepers.

An eleventh hour injury to Brown brought Haffey into direct competition with an England forward line at the height of its form. Bobby Robson opened the scoring, and by half-time England were winning 3–0; within minutes of the restart Scotland had pulled the game back to 3–2, and then the proverbial roof caved in. A Jimmy

One past Haffey

Frank Haffey finally gets a grip

Greaves hat-trick and two goals each from Bobby Smith and Jimmy Haynes left Scotland reeling from its worst ever defeat.

The next day the headlines gloated with the kind of effusive unction that only the English press could muster. "This was slaughter in the spring sunshine," wrote the *Sunday Express*; next to the report were nine horrific photographs, each one showing the tragic Frank Haffey in poses of utter desperation as he dived, slid and fumbled his way through the afternoon.

When the whistle blew to end the Scottish agony, Haffey left the field with his head bowed in a mixture of humiliation and loneliness. Scotland fans crowded at the entrance to Wembley threatening to lynch the keeper, and in an act of sad resignation, Haffey was forced to hide in a suburban house near the stadium. As the Scotland fans dispersed in shame, heading for the bars of Soho and the long train journey home, they created one of the country's most enduring jokes.

"What's the time? Nearly ten past Haffey!"

History was cruel to Frank Haffey. He is remembered for the Wembley disaster and little else, but the following season he inspired a poor Celtic team to pursue Dundee and Rangers for the League flag. In more than one crunch game when the pressure was off and the ball was in the opposition's half, Frank would climb on to the bar and endear himself to the Celtic faithful by pretending to sleep on the woodwork. But an unbelievable blunder at Airdrie in March 1962 ended the Parkhead challenge. Grabbing defeat from the jaws of victory, Haffey let in a shot it seemed easier to save.

The unforgiving finger of fate always seemed to single out Frank Haffey but eventually the fall guy had his day. The following season he was Celtic's star player in a memorable cup final when his heroic saves and faultless display of goalkeeping held the great Rangers side of the early '60s to a 1–1 draw. Rangers won the replay but the final became known as 'Haffey's Day'. It helped a little but could never erase the bitterness of the nine England goals. As if running away from his own mind the tragic Haffey emigrated to Australia where Scottish exiles still see him as a figure of unrivalled fun.

In September 2001, as Scotland were being horsed out of the World Cup by Belgium at the King Bedouin Stadium, Haffey's 9–3 jersey was auctioned on the Internet. Most of the bidders wished to remain anonymous.

Jim Leighton had the safest pair around. He was a victim of a land so accustomed to blaming goalkeepers that deep in his heart he even began to blame himself

Fumbling balls

The image of the disastrous goalkeeper has haunted Scottish football for the last 30 years. In some respects it is a misnomer. The keeper is an obvious fall guy, a last line of lonely defence whose faults and deficiencies are easy to expose. But Scotland has added to the disastrous image in the most masochistic ways.

In May 1975, at Wembley, the site of Haffey's worst nightmare, Scotland entrusted the role of goalkeeper to Stewart Kennedy, a keeper of such startling mediocrity that many Scotland fans believed it was only his association with Rangers that led to him being chosen. His performance was pitiful, five goals flew past him from a bewildering array of angles, and in one pathetic ritual he ended up wrapped round the goal-post in a knot of utter hopelessness.

Three years later in a midweek international against Wales, a look of solitary bewilderment was written on the face of Coventry City's Jim Blyth. Playing one of his few games in goal for Scotland, the keeper rolled the ball out to the experienced Manchester City fullback Willie Donachie; with a shot of slide-rule perfection, Donachie lobbed the ball back over the stranded Blyth, scoring a perfect own goal which gave Wales a fortunate draw. Blyth, exposed to the cruelty of a Hampden crowd tired of goalkeeping

ineptitude, wandered through the rest of his career with a guilt complex, another victim of the big-match blunder.

But when it comes to fumbling balls there are very few Scottish keepers who can rival the Norwich City custodian Bryan Gunn. According to salacious press reports he was unfairly implicated in what the tabloids refer to as "a three-in-the-bed" scandal. The incident reportedly happened in Hollywood in 1989 and involved Gunn and another Norwich player. A newspaper report claimed the players "staged a sex orgy in a Beverly Hills hotel with a beautician". Although Scottish goalkeepers have been accused of all sorts of malpractice, until Bryan Gunn's intervention, troilism had not been one of them. Gunn's most vociferous defender was his own father. "He's just a healthy young lad, I don't know what he gets up to in his sex life," he told the leering press. The incident did little harm to Gunn's career and in many respects endeared him to Scotland fans. In a country so used to dismal performances the prospect of a player scoring with such consummate style was rare indeed.

One of Scotland's smallest-ever keepers, the diminutive Rangers and Third Lanark custodian Jock Robertson will go down in history as a scapegoat with a sore head. John Greig, the Rangers captain during

Robertson's spell with Third Lanark, takes great pleasure in recounting an infamous tale during a New Year game at Brockville. Wee Jocky was apparently steaming after a particularly hospitable Hogmanay and played a blinder. Unfortunately for Third Lanark's dwindling support, he sobered up at half-time and duly let in five goals.

Next in line

The mantle of scapegoat was passed down through Scotland's goalkeeping history from Martin to Haffey, to Kennedy to Rough and then to the most unlikely scapegoat, the Aberdeen and Manchester United goalkeeper Jim Leighton. For years, Leighton seemed to have ended Scotland's fixation with goal-keeping disasters. Throughout the '80s he had been a tower of strength as the last line in defence and had single-handedly reversed the image of the inept Scottish keeper. History never had the heart to tell him that great keepers use both hands.

Jim Leighton, a product of Johnstone in Renfrewshire, established his reputation with Aberdeen where he won league and cup medals and was a rock solid member of Aberdeen's European Cup Winner's Cup team. He rose to become the most capped goalkeeper in the history of Scottish football and was chosen to represent Scotland in three consecutive World Cup Finals.

Leighton's fortunes changed when he left Aberdeen to rejoin Alex Ferguson at Manchester United. His form fluctuated in front of a porous and unconvincing Manchester United defence and his Scotland place was endangered by the form of the ex-Oldham and Hibernian keeper Andy Goram. When he least needed a vote of no confidence, Leighton was sensationally dropped from Manchester

United's 1990 Cup Final replay team and punished for a slump in form during a suspect season in front of a United defence that bordered on the arthritic.

Psychologically scarred by missing the replay, haunted by press humiliation and troubled by conceding a soft goal in the final World Cup qualifying game against Norway at Hampden, Leighton joined the Scotland squad in Italy. He was down but not out.

In an act of admirable but ultimately misguided loyalty, the national coach Andy Roxburgh stood by his dispirited keeper. After an indifferent

A jersey only a mother could knit

game against Costa Rica and an inspirational performance against Sweden when he saved Scotland's skin on several occasions, Leighton's luck finally ran out. In Scotland's 1–0 defeat by Brazil he was noticeably slow to respond in the run up that led to Brazil's winning goal and was unfairly attacked by the press. Once again a Scottish keeper was cast in the role of the disastrous fool.

Leighton was in many respects an unconvincing scapegoat. The history books will show he had an admirable career. Towards the end of his career, playing for Dundee and Hibernian, and exchanging the Scotland jersey with Andy Goram, Leighton began to take on the appearance of a haunted man.

His front teeth were false and when he played without them his incisors pointed downwards like a vampire. The image was too tempting – Leighton was nicknamed Dracula and we all know he was scared of crosses. He wore contact lenses on the pitch but off the field preferred a pair of wire rime glasses, which accentuated the belief that he was half-blind. His legs were outrageously bandy – wide enough for a loose ball to squirm through.

For Jim Leighton it ended in *diminuendo*. He was steretchered off the pitch after a few minutes of the Scottish Cup final against Rangers to be replaced by Aberdeen teammate Robbie Winters. And this after a bizarre episode in which he had been invited to join the Scotland squad as coach, in the week his biography was to be published. It was not the kindest book and did not paint team boss Craig Brown in a great light.

But in a history of disasters stretching across 30 years, Scotland has been plagued by calamity, lapses in concentration and self-induced tragedy. The goalkeeper is always to blame and

always will be. But in a land of careless hands, Jim Leighton had the safest pair around. He was a victim of a land so accustomed to blaming goalkeepers that deep in his heart he even began to blame himself.

Rough justice

Football fans can be vindictive. They can be sadistic. And on a big day when there's a trophy at stake or a local derby with old scores to settle, they can make the Marquis De Sade look like a good guy.

Picture this particular scene. It is a warm Saturday towards the end of the 1989–90 season, leagues are being decided, the unfortunates are being relegated and Scotland's itinerant football fans are weaving their way to the citadels of Brechin, Forfar and Cowdenbeath. Among the happiest band of travellers are 5,000 St Johnstone fans heading for the seaside and a match against Ayr United that will decide the First Division Championship.

Two points away from winning the First Division flag, Christmas has come early to the Perth fans. The opposition are under Ally McLeod's managerial direction and in his infinite wisdom, Ally has returned to the repressed traumas of Argentina by selecting Alan Rough in goal.

By perverse chance, in the days running up to the match Rough had been cruelly – and wrongly – accused of stealing meat from a local supermarket. To the delight of the away fans, an unexpected victim is between the posts and a new song has entered their vocal repertoire. As St Johnstone won by two goals their fans sang a song to the tune of *My Darling Clementine* – "Where's the mincemeat, where's the mincemeat Alan Rough? Its in your pocket, it's in your pocket, it's in your pocket Alan Rough."

The loyal joker

Alan Rough was born and bred in the Gorbals in Glasgow and had his upbringing in a closely-knit family that supported the prodigal son from Ballater Street Primary School, to Partick Thistle Amateurs and ultimately to the Scottish international team.

On 17 April 1990, the *Daily Record* broke the news that Alan Rough had been charged in connection with £5 of meat taken from an Ayr supermarket. He was allegedly detained at the town's Safeway supermarket after a Friday afternoon shopping expedition went wrong. Police were called and Rough was later charged with the theft of butcher meat.

In what must rank as the most offal moment in the history of Hampden Babylon, the paper reported the words of a senior Strathclyde police spokesman:

"We can confirm that a 38-year-old-man is the subject of a report to the procurator fiscal. This follows a charge of shoplifting of an amount of meat from an Ayr superstore." The amount of meat was never specified, but football fans throughout Scotland had no doubts, it must have been Caledonia's most famous culinary repast: a pund o' mince.

Alan Rough is the typical antihero. Although he stumbled into football as much by accident as design, he rose to become one of Scotland's most charismatic players. In a career that began at Partick Thistle and included spells with Hibernian, Celtic, Ayr United and Orlando Lions, he briefly held the record as Scotland's most-capped goalkeeper and played more than 800 games in a career spanning 18 years.

It is to Rough's eternal credit that he developed a sense of humour, which carried him through experiences that ranged from the sublime to the ridiculous. He was a dressing-room joker, a

"Whaur's yer Peru when it's cauld?"

loyal club player and an outstanding international despite the inevitable victimisation he suffered as one of football's most put upon figures, the Scottish goalkeeper. But the false - accusations of shoplifting devastated the player and his family and have left him bitter about the way Scottish newspapers pursue the private lives of football's master race.

By his own admission, Rough is one of football's midnight runners. On two occasions, he was soaked to the skin when the Scotland manager Jock Stein caught him out. Humiliation was at the centre of Jock Stein's disciplinary philosophy. Rather than send a player home in disgrace and implicate the footballer's family in a public scandal, Stein preferred the football

By his own admission, Rough is one of football's midnight runners

equivalent of a damn good caning and used to enjoy throwing a drink over offending players.

On one occasion before a match against Northern Ireland in a high security hotel in Ireland, Rough joined a journalist for a quiet drink. He ordered coke but unknown to Rough the journalist laced the drink with a stiff dram. Stein came along, smelt the drink, refused to listen to Rough's explanation, picked up the glass and threw it at the keeper and marched off.

In the run-up to a Home International game at Hampden, the Scotland squad was assembled at a hotel in Troon. Always in search of alternative entertainment, Rough led the team's other two keepers George Wood and David Harvey on a late-night expedition to a local hostelry known as The Marine Grill. In time honoured tradition, the players returned well after the curfew time had expired. For once they managed to evade the searchlights, dodge the

guard-dogs, tunnel under the barbed wire and make it back to the sanctuary of their bunks before Stein and the Stalag Squad knew they were gone.

It was a great escape for a team so used to getting caught, but Rough and his fellow revellers chanced their luck and noisily ordered room service when they got back to the hotel. The sandwiches were quickly followed by the wrath of the Scotland manager, who charged into the bedroom and threw a glass of milk over the startled keeper. Rough was made to face the ultimate humiliation the next morning. He was forced to train until he was physically sick.

Rough was lucky to miss out on one of Scottish football's most infamous scandals, when he missed the taxi that whisked five of his international team-mates to the notorious bender in Copenhagen which led to them being banned for life. In fact, luck played tricks with Alan Rough throughout his career. He was discovered playing on a local works pitch in Glasgow's Anniesland, when a Patrick Thistle and Manchester United scout stumbled on the game after another local match was cancelled. He made his international debut in April 1976 against Switzerland and once again luck played its part. The first-choice keeper, David Harvey of Leeds United, called off in what remain the most unlikely circumstances in the history of the game. Harvey had a farm in Yorkshire and two of the cows were about to give birth.

Look no telly!

If luck was kind to Alan Rough it also paid him a monstrous disservice. His career was riddled with spectacular match winning saves and unbelievable calamities. When Scotland played Wales at Liverpool in the dramatic World Cup qualifier, he miraculously pushed a John Toshack lob onto the

Rough was hardly a product of the Harvard Business School. Money passed through his hands with the slippery insecurity of a wet ball

bar, a save that turned the game in Scotland's favour and set the seal on Scotland's trip to Argentina.

At a party after the match, the Aberdeen striker Joe 'The Budgie' Harper led a vocal and very eventful celebration party. When Rough returned home to Glasgow the CID swooped on his house trying to recover a colour television set that had been stolen from the hotel. Rough was innocent, but his endearing biography leaves a shadow of doubt over the innocence of other Scots who were in Liverpool on that famous night.

Towards the end of his playing career Rough was with Hibs and contemplating a move to the Orlando Lions, a short-lived soccer team in Florida. His business interests not only brought him appalling bad luck but imposed a series of financial setbacks that were to affect him in the years to come. Like many footballers at the twilight of their careers, Rough looked round for a suitable business interest and eventually opened his own shop in Musselburgh. He may have been an outstanding goalkeeper but he was hardly a product of the Harvard Business School. Money passed through his hands with the slippery insecurity of a wet ball.

By April 1990, when over a third of the Scottish populace was avoiding the poll tax, Alan Rough had his own reasons for fearing a Warrant Sale. At the eleventh hour he managed to prevent a sheriff's officer from taking goods from his home to pay off outstanding business debts. Just when it looked like the proverbial music centre was to disappear out the front door and into the sheriff's van, Rough managed to contact his solicitors who paid the £250 Rough owed to an Edinburgh sports company. "It's all very embarrassing, but that's me in the clear now," said a relieved Rough. It was his third warrant sale scare in six months.

After a nerve-wracking and mentally exhausting three months, complicated by a threat of sequestration proceedings brought by the Marine Highland Hotel for an alleged unpaid bill of £750, Rough's career continued on a downward spiral. He left Ayr to become player-coach of junior side Glenafton for a fee of £1,000 and less than £100 per match.

Anyone can make a mistake

Alan Rough has given more to Scottish football than he could ever take and for that reason alone he stands on the terraces of Hampden Babylon like a colossus. Not only is he one of the best goalkeepers the country ever produced, but the only Scottish internationalist who can honestly claim he was involved in the mysterious case of the missing meat. If TV's investigative programme *Rough Justice* was to test its forensic mettle on Ayrshire meat Alan Rough would get off scot-free.

In an unusually tender story, which appeared in the *Sun*'s soaraway issue of 3 August 1990, Alan Rough was allowed the dignity of a personal reply to the charges, which 12 weeks later would be dropped. He told the paper that his life had been a torment after his arrest and explained that a simple error had led to his misfortune.

Rough told how his wife Michelle had taught him to keep fresh food away from detergents. "I was careful to put the bleach in the front of the trolley and the meat at the back," he explained. "But as I was packing the stuff into a carrier bag at the checkout I missed the butcher meat and sat a carrier bag on top of it by mistake."

And there's no doubt that in the lonely life of a Scottish goalkeeper, mistakes can happen. ◊

7

BREMNER BLAMES BLONDES

Modern British history is riddled with miscarriages of justice. The trials of the Birmingham Six and the Guildford Four provide damning evidence of the state's corrupt disregard for the rights of innocent people unfortunate enough to be caught in the wrong place at the wrong time with the wrong kind of Irish accent.

But it would be naive in the extreme to believe that the system is always unjust – as evidence I present the case of a notorious bunch of Scottish footballers now known as the Copenhagen Five.

On the night of 9 September 1975, during a long and contentious meeting at the SFA's headquarters, the case of the Copenhagen Five was heard *in camera*. Like a Presbyterian version of *Judge Dredd*, the association's assistant secretary, Ernie Walker, solemnly placed a black cap on his head and passed sentence. Five players were found guilty of bringing the game into serious disrepute and banned for life. In the most draconian punishment ever handed out to Scottish internationalists, Billy Bremner, Joe Harper, Pat McCluskey, Willie Young and Arthur Graham were told they would never play for their country again.

It must have been some bender!

When Anne Simonsen set out to work at the Marina Hotel in

Sad end to Bremner's international career

by JOHN RAFFERTY

The international committee of the Scottish Football Association will this afternoon investigate reports of indiscipline among players in the Scotland party which won two matches in Denmark last week.

Willie Ormond has been called to the meeting. Mr Allan said: " We will hear the team manager and find out what he knows about the events. If he can give us authoritative information then we will take action on that. If not, then we will hold another meeting and call to it the players who have been named."

The players who have been named are Billy Bremner and Joe Harper, of the full team, and Willie Young, Arthur Graham, and Pat McCluskey of Under-23 squad. There was trouble over a bill in a club in Copenhagen in the early hours Thursday and the police had to be called.

Later there was some trouble in the room of an SFA guest in the team hotel. There was some disarrangement of the furnishings and a blow was struck and Bremner was hit.

The evening started quietly and the players had a meal when they returned from the match on Wednesday. They played at Copenhagen but stayed at Vedbaek. The meal was finished shortly after 11 p.m. and they were given permission by Willie Ormond to stay out till 1 a.m.

The training staff waited and checked the whole party in before the deadline and then they went to bed contented. But five players — Bremner, Harper, Young, Graham and McCluskey — went out again and went into Copenhagen, 15 miles away. They were welcomed at a club where Bremner was known but the mood changed when the bill was presented.

The police were called when the situation became unpleasant. They cleared the trouble but their intervention was recorded in a police report and in a small story in a local newspaper. Before the police arrived, Arthur Graham had left the party and returned to Vedbaek by taxi.

The others returned later to the hotel and then there was the incident in the room of an SFA guest. Next morning, the managers, Willie Ormond and Jimmy Bonthrone, and the trainers were astonished to learn that there was something amiss. They had expected a peaceful night when they had checked in the players and especially since there was no centre of temptation within 15 miles.

The international committee have authoritative information about what happened in the hotel room but they may have to wait until they interview the players before they know what happened at the club in Copenhagen. They, of course, know

mittee now must be seen take the correct action establish this."

Mr Rankin Grimshaw, president of the SFA, s: " We must remember that these are not dealing with k: These are men who have responsibility to themselves, their families, to their cl and to their country. It dreadful that players can di: gard these ethics. Th players were put on trust bt am afraid that can ne happen again."

Billy Bremner for sure brought to an end his in national career and just w he was within two caps breaking the record in national appearances for a ! set by Denis Law. He was volved in another dawn e pade with Jimmy Johnstone Largs and survived because it was thought that presence in West Germany essential to the success of Scotland team.

Billy Bremner said night: " The story that I h been involved in a fight absolute rubbish. Talk ol fight is ridiculous. I deny anything like this happened

"One day we'll be managers and the bastards will be in bed by ten"

A draw against Iran and getting beat by Costa Rica are indignity enough, but a star player assaulting a policeman with a Hush Puppy is testing fan loyalty to the limit

Copenhagen where she had a job as part-time barmaid, it seemed like just another night. The reception staff had told her the Scottish football team was in residence in the hotel. Naively, she imagined it increased her hopes of picking up the odd tip in order to ease her way through University. The last thing on her mind was that she would end the evening being drenched with a glass of rum and coke and would become the femme fatale in a low-budget 'B' movie called *Hampden Babylon.*

It was downstairs in the hotel's night-bar that the unfortunate Ms Simonsen met her undignified match. In a front-page story entitled 'Blonde Blames Bremner', the *Daily Record* reported that the hotel's assistant manager, Lars Borch, was attempting to calm a group of noisy Scottish players down, when he heard a chant of "One, two, three …" He watched in disbelief as Bremner, taking the captain's role, reportedly drenched the barmaid with a glass of drink.

"I am not a football fan," said Ms Simonsen, shaken but not stirred. "Bremner spoke to me earlier but I just ignored him. I don't know whether it was because I ignored him that he threw the drink over me," she added.

Ironically, a few days earlier, when Simonsen heard that the Scottish team was at the hotel, she had told a friend it was an ideal opportunity to brush up on her English. An evening in the company of William Bremner, one of the Raploch's least-gifted linguists, was hardly the ideal night-school.

The plucky Simonsen, not accustomed to being on the wrong end of a double Bacardi, took a principled feminist stance, complained to the management and insisted that the local police were called. It was the phone call that blew the whistle on one of Scottish football's biggest blowouts, a night of post-match revelry which will be warmly remembered under the heading, "Five Go Mad In Denmark".

According to police files in Copenhagen, the five players treated

Scandinavia to the seamier side of Scottish culture. It was an evening of song and celebration. The Aberdeen striker Joe Harper scored the only goal in a hard-fought international against Denmark, and the Scots set out to party.

In their infinite wisdom, the SFA had arranged for a Scotland Under-23 side to travel with the senior squad, in the admirable belief that it would be a

learning experience for the young stars of the future.

It was.

Three of the younger players, Willie Young and Arthur Graham of Aberdeen and the Celtic sweeper Pat McCluskey were all members of a Scotland team that had won the night before in Frederikshavn. They learned to their cost the subtle art of starting a rammy in a Danish disco.

Billy Bremner led by example. The wee ginger-haired midfielder who was once described as "a volcano looking for somewhere to explode", took his men on a drinking spree that stretched from the downstairs bar of the Marina Hotel to an exclusive Copenhagen nightclub called Bonapartes. And then back again.

As the entourage stalked the streets of Scandinavia, they left a toll of chaos in their wake. The police were called to Bonapartes after customers complained of rowdy behaviour. When they arrived, they discovered the five Scots in various stages of alcoholic disrepair. The barman on that fateful evening had the unfortunate name of Bent Dorf a moniker that the poor man would not comfortably explain in a Scottish supporters' club.

Soft shoe scuffle

Bent claimed that customers were appalled by the bad behaviour of the Scotland squad and that when he asked for order they threatened to punch out his lights. By this time Pat McCluskey's sense of balance was not of the required athletic standard and the police were called. An eyewitness claims that at the height of the commotion, McCluskey motioned to hit a policeman and had to be physically restrained. As the other four offered their own inimitable advice, the police hustled the Celtic defender downstairs and out into the streets where he was thrown over the bonnet of a police car.

Bremner's feet go one way, his body another

Not content to go quietly, McCluskey took off his shoe and threatened the Danish cops with a sound thrashing. It was at this critical moment that good sense got the better of the others, Big Pat was calmed down and a semblance of order was restored. It is with a huge sigh of relief that Scottish football fans can reflect on this crucial moment. A draw against Iran and getting beat by Costa Rica are indignity enough, but a star player assaulting a policeman with a Hush Puppy is testing fan loyalty to the limit.

Copenhagen was a turning point in Pat McCluskey's career. With the stigma of a life-ban hanging over him, his club form never realised its early potential and he ended up working as a storeman on an offshore oil rig.

Fortunately, the Danish polis had imbibed the peaceful spirit of Mahatma Ghandi. Fearing the arrests might cause an embarrassing international incident, they merely lectured the five Scots and allowed them to weave their way back into the night, to more drink and more disruption.

As the night grew older incidents multiplied. Manager Willie Ormond's 1 am curfew was not simply broken, it was annihilated. The five players returned to the hotel's night-bar, where they had been asked to calm down earlier in the night. A member of the SFA council Jock McDonald had his hotel bedroom wrecked and rumours of a punch-up were rife.

Billy Bremner played a captain's part.

If FIFA ever gets round to creating an identikit picture of national football stereotypes, the Scottish player will be short, stocky, aggressive and ginger haired. He will have a fiery temper, a bad disciplinary record and a passionate spirit. He will come from a rough housing scheme in Stirling and his name will be Billy Bremner.

An enduring myth is that Scotland loves bad boys and England feels safer with creeps

An odd-looking miniature ginger-haired fearsome animal poses with a model of a lion

Who's afraid of the tiger?

Bremner was a Scottish Schoolboy captain and signed for Leeds as a teenager, arriving at Elland Road soon after another young Scottish star: East Fife's Henry McLeish, who decades later became the First Minister in the devolved Scottish Parliament.

Even in his teens Bremner stamped his authority on games, pursuing players until they made mistakes and bullying those around him into raising their game. Although he never grew much above five foot five, Bremner was always in the thick of disputes and played according to the old motto, 'When the going gets tough, the tough get going.'

One famous photograph from the past captures a rare moment of fear when the impetuous Bremner, playing an early game for Leeds United, is threatened by an even tougher adversary, the Spurs and Scotland halfback Dave 'Tiger' Mackay. Had the two been at their prime in the same era Scotland's midfield would have made Dirty Harry look like a wimp.

During his first ten seasons as a professional, Bremner lost almost half a season through misconduct. He was banned five times between 1964 and 1967 but his flexibility as a player was such that Bremner played as a winger and a sweeper for Leeds United before he became the club's midfield dynamo. He won his first Scottish cap in 1965 against Spain by which time he was known as "the prince of nigglers", and one of the most unruly players in the professional game. Bremner once tried to rile an opponent by drawing attention to his pock-marked face by shouting "Go and get it filled in with polyfilla", but the crunch came when he was sent off in 1967 for fouling the Nottingham Forest 'keeper Peter Grummitt. Manager and mentor Don Revie lost patience with Bremner and demanded he keep his temper in check.

Five Go Mad in Denmark

For several years it looked like Bremner had calmed down, the excessive niggling was controlled and the bristling temper was kept on a leash, but trouble was always brooding just beneath the surface. When he was voted the English League's Player of the Year in 1973, the *Sunday Telegraph* marvelled at his new maturity, and described his

transformation as being "like Attila the Hun giving up fighting for sculpture". They spoke too soon; Attila Bremner had his eyes on the prize.

Cuffing Kev

One of the great distinctions that can be drawn between football culture in Scotland and England is in the public's attitude to heroes. With the recent and spectacular exceptions of Paul Gascoigne and the sozzled dreariness of Tony Adams, England's heroes have been consistently straight. Whilst England favours sterling and upstanding professionals like Billy Wright, Bobby Charlton and Gary Lineker, Scotland has traditionally lionised the anti-heroes, players like Alex James, Jim Baxter, Jimmy Johnstone and Mo Johnston, men who seem to be at war with authority and traumatised by their exceptional skills.

"Being bollocked by Billy is a bit hard to take. It's a bit like Dean Martin telling you to stop drinking"

An enduring myth that separates football across the border is that Scotland loves bad boys and England feels safer with creeps. In the creep-show of English international football the man most Scots loved to hate was a perm-headed striker who went by the name of Kevin Keegan. Beloved by the English media and blessed with the irritating air of a professional nice guy, Keegan was the ultimate 'yes' man. He was not only destined to play for England but to manage them too.

In the eyes of Scots fans everywhere, he needed a good doing, and if Tiger Mackay was too old to give him one, then there was always Wild Bill Bremner.

Billy Bremner seemed unable to do things by half. At the height of the club rivalry between Leeds United and Liverpool, he chose the showpiece Charity Cup Final of 1974 to vent a nation's revenge on Keegan. After a series of physical exchanges in which Bremner rarely came second, the ref-

eree detected that the increasing levels of animosity were about to spoil the game as a spectacle and sent both Bremner and Keegan for an early bath.

Disgusted with their treatment, the two players tore off their shirts and threw them to the ground in full view of the royal box. They were banned and fined £500 for bringing the game into disrepute. The Wembley 'square go' was more of a blot on Keegan's copybook than on the already soiled jotters of William Bremner. As a Scottish paper remarked at the time, it was not his first dismissal: "Bremner has had more early baths than a miner on night-shift."

Managing failure

In a career that was both long and eventful, Bremner played 770 games for Leeds United and characterised the team's tough-tackling professional image. His drive and energy helped Leeds to four FA cup finals and two league titles, before he moved to nearby Hull City where he played another 61 games. He won 52 caps for Scotland but there is no doubt that a mixture of club commitments and the carry-on in Copenhagen prevented him from winning many more.

Bremner is one of many Scottish players who made a remarkable transformation when he took up a career in management. Like Tommy Docherty at Manchester United, Graeme Souness at Rangers, Alex Ferguson at Aberdeen and Alex McDonald at Hearts and Airdrie, he became a born-

again disciplinarian, a man with a short memory when it came to chastising those who misbehaved. One Scottish player who played under Bremner when he managed Leeds, said, "Being bollocked by Billy is a bit hard to take. Its a bit like Dean Martin telling you to stop drinking."

Despite being fined £500 for making foul and abusive comments to match officials whilst managing Doncaster Rovers, Bremner wielded a rod of discipline and rarely bothered to reflect on his image as a rogue newly attuned to respectability. The roots of his disciplinarian style go back a long way. He was a tough and uncompromising player with a hard man image but he was also a supremely loyal competitor who stayed with Leeds at a time when a big money transfer might have been more lucrative.

Bremner was never a 'mercenary' player, but he believed implicitly in 'player power' and acted as the dressing-room shop steward for Leeds and Scotland. His style was always demanding, hustling and manipulative. In one memorable outburst at Leeds, he once made a plea for more money, claiming that professional footballers were little more than 'white slaves'. At club level, his persistent niggling paid off, but at international level it often acted as a destabilising influence, and may well have led to the premature departure of Willie Ormond as the national team manager.

Thrown to the wolves

Bremner was a midfield bandit willing to stretch the referee's tolerance to breaking point, but football was his personal code of honour. A series of scathing and ultimately unfounded articles published in the *Sunday People* accusing him of bribery led to a High Court appearance and an early end to his playing career. It was a press vilification that deeply injured Bremner's sense of personal integrity and, like a tackle from behind, he refused to take it lying down.

The bribery scandal sickened Bremner. In an ill-advised piece of muck-raking the newspaper printed comments by two former Wolves players, the ex-Irish internationalist Danny Hegan and the former Scotland defender Frankie Munro. Both told the *People* that Bremner had offered them bribes before and during a crucial league decider between Leeds United and Wolves at the end of the season in 1972. The sums varied. The witnesses claimed in their evidence that Hegan was the poor relation, he was reputedly offered £1,000, and swore he heard Bremner say "Give us a penalty and I'll give you a grand." Munro was more upmarket. According to the evidence he was offered five grand.

The highly publicised court case brought unwelcome notoriety to Bremner, casting a shadow of doubt over his career and causing untold misery to his family. From his home in Maltby in Yorkshire, he told journalists that the accusations had devastated his children. "It was terrible," he said, "my children were taunted at school with 'your father is a fixer' and my wife got reactions going shopping." In his final few league games, Bremner was taunted unmercifully by rival fans. Always a figure of abuse from the terracing, the taunts of "fixer", "cheat" and "bribing bastard" brought a level of loathing that he found unacceptable.

Bremner's decision to sue the *Sunday People* by taking out a libel action against the paper's owners and Hegan was an attempt to clear his name and retrieve his integrity rather than a money-making scheme. But Bremner's subsequent court victory brought in £100,000 in damages, more

"Joe, I know you play for the jersey, but does it have to be that one?"

than a testimonial at Elland Road would ever have reaped.

The law was on Bremner's side and the evidence painted Hegan and Munro in a sleazy light. At the time of the trial, Hegan was living in Coatbridge and earning a pittance as a Butlins' Redcoat and Munro was living in Australia. The hearing admitted he had only agreed to appear in court if his wife and children were flown back to Britain with him at the cost of £4,000.

It was Frankie Munro's holiday in hell. Munro was a player who might easily have been with Bremner and company had he been with Scotland when the Copenhagen Five went daft. Facing his fellow countryman across a courtroom had the same tainted divisiveness as the day Tommy Docherty faced his Manchester United prodigy

Willie Morgan in the Old Bailey.

After an inevitable return to Leeds United for a brief spell as manager, his old club finally sacked him. Bremner's dismissal came at a critical period for Leeds, when the hooligan element within the club's support had brought them widespread contempt. Typically, Bremner hated the hooligans and demanded heavy punitive action against what he had described as "the moronic mob", but ironically the image that Leeds had fashioned over the years owed as much to his barbed-wire aggressiveness as the behaviour of the fans.

Leeds supporters have terrorised most of England but they weren't around on the night the volcano erupted and five went mad in Copenhagen.

Fun in the Sun

The Copenhagen Five set standards that few Scotland teams have matched. But many before and since have understood that the nation has high expectations of the low moral standards of Scottish footballers on tour.

Argentina registered a hurricane on the rammy scale. In fact there were so many sporadic and incongruous bust-ups that it would take a military historian to catalogue the complexities of the manoeuvres that the Scotland squad embarked on.

Such was the fallout from 1978 that it wasn't until the summer of 1990 that another Scottish World Cup squad were to even try to match the Copenhagen Five. And it was a pretty poor attempt.

Andy Roxburgh's Scotland squad headed for Genoa and the opening stages of the 1990 World Cup. By a mixture of luck and national destiny, Scotland based themselves at the fashionable Bristol Hotel, an elegant resort hotel in Rappallo overlooking the picturesque Ligurian coastline.

Something should have clicked at the SFA.

After a lifetime of incidents by the sea, the idea of housing a Scotland international football team in a lively holiday resort is about as advisable as sending Warren Beatty to a nunnery. The inevitable happened with familiar consequences.

The Italia World Cup campaign coincided with a tense circulation war between the *Daily Record*, Scotland's biggest selling paper, and its belligerent new rival the *Sun*. Flushed by the success of breaking the 'Mo signs for Gers' story, the *Sun* embarked on an adventurous and aggressive campaign to find scoops in the Scotland camp.

It was hardly the most daunting task in journalism.

Scotland's World Cup campaign was a disaster with a difference. Frustrated

"Anyone seen Danny Hegan?"

by past embarrassments and determined that the squad would not be visited by the mismanagement and inflated hype of past campaigns, the SFA with the meticulous ex-school-teacher Andy Roxburgh at the helm, travelled to Italy with dignity and decorum. Unfortunately, the team came along with them.

In a nightmare of a game that made Argentina look like good fun, Scotland stumbled at the first hurdle against lowly Costa Rica. Scapegoats were thick on the ground, very few players reached their true potential. Mo Johnston had been unusually

quiet and the Aberdeen midfield player Jim Bett – the erstwhile invisible man – was conspicuous by his inactivity.

The day after the match, the *Sun* in Scotland led with an incriminating article headlined "Scots Stars in Champagne Booze-up". For most fans it was a case of *déjà-vu*; here was the archetypal Scottish disaster story being rewritten for the umpteenth time; a diabolical performance against an unfancied team followed by a sordid revelation of scandal behind the scenes.

But this time the story came with an unusual moral twist: true or false?

The *Sun*'s report was crammed full of unattributed sources, hearsay and speculation. It involved Jim Bett, the player most Scotland fans had singled out as the scapegoat in the game against Costa Rica, and Mo Johnston, probably the most harassed figure in the modern history of the Scottish game. The article claimed that Johnston and Bett had turned up at a local restaurant with two Scottish girls and in a deft tactical switch left with "two Italian lovelies on their arms".

The players denied the story had any

newshounds that Johnston and Bett had returned to the hotel in time and that no curfew had been broken.

Although the *Sun* was keen to titillate their readers with a hint of sex, it was undoubtedly that seductive temptress called 'bevvy' that gave the story its bite. In Scotland's Italia '90 campaign drink had become a moral barometer and, anxious that the mistakes of previous generations would not be rekindled, Roxburgh had gone to great lengths to set out a code of conduct around alcohol.

break of hooliganism, the Italian authorities banned the sale of alcohol on the day of matches. Never convinced of the merits of sobriety, it was a challenge that Scotland's Tartan Army met with considerable ingenuity. A whole array of strategies were tried out – drink was stored in hotel rooms for days, bottles of mineral water smelt suspiciously like Bacardi, oranges were injected with vodka and many Scotland fans drank a cheap wine that Italians use instead of vinegar. The grocers of Genoa sold it openly never imagining that someone would drink the stuff. But the roving army swaying towards the Luigi Ferraris Stadium had already dusted down an old Wembley favourite and sang "You Cannae Ban Us Fae Bevvy".

The ban on drinks introduced a delicate morality to the 1990 World Cup. The fans were expected to calm down and the players were watched like hawks. Only the press itself seemed to be above the moral law. By day Scotland's journalists dipped their pens in moral authority as they complained about Bett and Johnston's big night out, by midnight many of them were propping up the bar in the Grand Hotel Miramar in such a state of disrepair that Mo Johnston was a choirboy by comparison.

One of the enduring facts of 'Scotland on Tour' is that despite the reckless reputation of the Tartan Army and the Copenhagen Five, neither fans nor players come remotely close to matching the debauched anarchy of Scotland's moralising journalists. When you are far from home, the pen is mightier than the sordid. Hypocrisy and media hype make a potent cocktail. ◊

> ## *The article claimed that Johnston and Bett had turned up at a local restaurant with two Scottish girls and in a deft tactical switch left with "two Italian lovelies on their arms"*

significant merit, and exhausted with being singled out by the media, Johnston threatened to take legal action. In a press conference at the Bristol Hotel, Andy Roxburgh closed ranks and defended his players by saying that no breach of discipline had taken place and that both Johnston and Bett had been given permission to have a drink. He rejected press speculation that team captain Roy Aitken had been hurriedly sent to collect the two players in a taxi, and assured the

The rod of discipline

In order to instil discipline in the ranks, Roxburgh had instituted a drinks ban on the players during Scotland's acclimatisation trip to Malta. Oddly enough, the ban also included under-arm deodorant – not because – as some cynics remarked – the squad were prone to snorting it, but because it prevented the process of sweating and dehydration and inhibited the physical preparation of the players. Much was made of the drinks ban in Malta and for very good reasons both the press and the fans were under the illusion that the ban would stay in effect until Scotland was knocked out of the World Cup.

Drinks bans were in vogue in Italy in the summer of 1990. Fearing an out-

8

WE HATE JIMMY HILL

Even Jimmy Hill's sexuality has a history. It began on a platform at Euston Station in 1928. A black American jazz band led them through the streets of London on a journey to dreamland where Hughie would play and England would falter.

Those that could afford to travel wore old great coats and Balmoral hats and the songs they sang were the quaint ballads of New Year and the rousing folk songs of rural Scot-land. They made their way by foot on the long walk to Wembley to watch the Wizards put five past England.

I'll say that again: *they made their way by foot on the long walk to Wembley to watch the wizards put five past England.*

Jazz bands, a bottle of Dewar's and stuffing the English. In the history of the Tartan Army, life doesn't come better than that. The history of the most bizarre fan base in football had begun in earnest,

There had been a sizeable and noisy travelling support dating back to the late nineteenth century, in the quaint old days when neither Rangers or Celtic existed and Vale of Leven used to rack up away wins.

But the term 'Tartan Army' is recent. In fact it was not until the 1970s, when gods like Jim Baxter and Denis Law had already retired, that the Scottish support adopted its infamous military name.

In the early part of that decade, when the Provisional IRA's bombing campaign was at its height, a small and largely insignificant Scottish terrorist group called the Tartan Army began bombing oil pipelines as a protest against the colonisation of Scotland by American, Dutch and English-based multinationals. They weren't too keen on the decline in macaroon bars either but that's another story.

The Tartan Army was loosely connected to the militant SNLA, the Scottish National Liberation Army. By Irish standards it was an inefficient and cranky setup, but the bombs did enough damage to frighten politicians and the oil industry. And the name hung around enough for the tabloids to cotton on.

The SNLA and the Tartan Army surfaced at a time when Scotland fans regularly besieged Wembley on their biannual trip to play England, in the ill-fated home internationals. Draped

Scotland fans were never slow to find the best bars in London

in lion rampant flags, sporting feather cuts and tartan flares, the Scotland support marched on Trafalgar Square leaving cans of Tartan Special lying in their wake.

Right-wing Conservative MP for Wembley Rhodes Boyson was one of the first public figures to object to Scotland fans, and once warned his constituents: "Lock up your daughters, the Jocks are coming." Fifteen years later, with Frank McAvennie and Charlie Nicholas on board, the daughters of Harrow and Wealdstone had

more to fear from the team bus than from the fans. But politicians like a demon and this time it stuck.

Here come the Jocks

The tabloid press greeted the Scotland support as a new folk-devil that could rekindle the memory of mods and rockers. But they needed a name to really catch on. The comparison with the half-arsed terrorists was too tempting for the press to avoid. Scotland fans became the 'Tartan Army' and it was a name they accepted

with wicked pride.

For over ten years, until English football hooliganism rose in earnest, the Tartan Army was the most feared group of football fans in Europe.

Changes in travel and transport played an important role in the rise of the Tartan Army. In the 1920s, when pioneer Scots travelled south to Wembley, the main mode of transport was the steam train. Railway workers, who benefited from 'PTs', the privilege tickets they received as part of their wages, made up the majority of travelling fans. To this day, Scotland still draws some of its most dedicated support from old railway towns like Motherwell, Larbert, Perth and Inverness.

Until the Fifties, railway workers were among the only working class people who could afford the trip to Wembley. No-one but the team travelled abroad, so the Scotland fans' fragile emotions were spared the ignominy of the World Cup finals in Switzerland in 1954, where not even captain Tommy Docherty could joke his way out of a 7–0 hammering by Uruguay.

By the Seventies, steam trains had disappeared to be replaced by the infamous 'football specials'. Hundreds of overnight trains left Scotland just before midnight carrying thousands of drunken fans south to London.

Many were members of the Scottish street gangs of the period: the Maryhill Fleet, the Calton Tongs and the Govan Team from Glasgow, the Shimmy and the Kirkton Huns from Dundee, the Niddrie Terror from Edinburgh and the Mental Pack from Perth.

The people of Carlisle and Crewe have good reason to remember these trains with disgust. Scotland fans were not a particularly pleasant bunch. England was enemy territory and years of inarticulate and pent up patriotism were thrown out of the broken

The trick was to squeeze enough fans on board to keep the petrol costs down, but leave enough room under the seats for the ubiquitous carry-out

By 1998 there was more chance of being bored to death by a Scot reciting Burns than a drunk spewing in your anorak pocket

Mel Gibson's barmy army, Paris 1998

Argentina campaign by submarine, while in 1998 a group of fans set sail from Oban to France. Docking rights were secured on the River Seine and the crew had registered the name 'The Tartan Navy'.

In 2001 when 12,000 Scots besieged Brussels in the fading days of Craig Brown's reign as Scotland boss, a group of fans travelled in a lovingly restored 1950s fire engine. Predictably, it was Scotland that ended up burned as Belgium booked their flight for the World Cup finals in Japan.

Today travel is not only more organised, it is more corporate and inextricably bound up in the controlled access to tickets. Street gangs have long since been outlawed and membership of the Scottish Travel Club is strictly controlled. Priority for tickets to matches overseas is carefully managed and the image of Scotland has been gradually transformed. By 1998 there was more chance of being bored to death by a Scot reciting Burns than a drunk spewing in your anorak pocket.

The vast majority of Scots with tickets for the prestigious World Cup opening match against Brazil in St Denis in 1998 had travelled to three or more of the qualifying matches, and in most cases were at the phantom game against Estonia in Tallinn, when only Scotland turned up.

That match has provoked one of the more endearing Tartan Army anthems – "One team in Tallinn, there's only one team in Tallinn." But aficionados of the Scotland chant refuse to believe that it's nearly as good as the old ones. It was cute, fun and self-mocking. I'd rather remember the threatening pathology of the 1970s: "Six-foot-two, eyes of blue, Big Jim Holton's after you."

Opposition to England will always beat strongly in the heart of the Tartan Army. For the most part it's healthy hatred, but there remains a warped

windows of the football specials as the Tartan Army headed south.

The 'specials' were invariably wrecked before they got close to London. In one particularly desperate bid to appease the Tartan Army, British Rail pioneered a disco-train – a carriage with piped pop music – where fans could dance away the journey together. Unfortunately, most preferred to scream abuse at people hanging out their washing in Peterborough and the experiment faded out. No more would the Tartan Army smooch

to Barry White, their handbags placed suspiciously on the floor.

Each invasion needs its own military strategy and so each major tournament has provoked a new response to travel. When British Rail banned football specials, the mini-bus became a Wembley institution. The trick was to squeeze enough fans on board to keep the petrol costs down, but leave enough room under the seats for the ubiquitous carry-out.

In 1978, members of the Tartan Army travelled to the ill-fated

The newly-pragmatic Tartan Army

minority whose resentment is barely disguised racism. The Tartan Army has always taken supreme pleasure in England's downfall.

Diego Maradona's infamous 'hand of God' goal frequently tops the list of Scottish supporters' all-time top goals. To this day, the Tartan Army pays homage to Diego with a song and dance routine loosely based on the hokey-cokey:

> "You put your right hand in,
> Your right hand out,
> In-out, in-out, shake it all about,
> You do the Maradona and
> You turn around,
> That's what it's all about,
> Oh Diego Maradona,
> He put the English out, out, out."

The Tartan Army is so accustomed to being filmed by the international media that ordinary fans have become self-obsessed

Masters of the song can also squeeze in the sound of a nose snorting cocaine just as the chorus comes round again. But it isn't easy and needs practice in front of the wardrobe mirror.

England's downfall is the reward the Tartan Army can always count on. In the run up to a major tournament, the English media can be relied on to exaggerate the prospects of their team.

For Scots, the sense of historic irritation is all the greater when the messengers are the BBC – the *British Broadcasting Corporation*.

Of poofs and presenters

For the Tartan Army the abiding memory of Euro '96 was not England's defeat itself, but the depressed faces of David Baddiel and

Frank Skinner as their new-lad party came to a sudden and brutal end. It is a video tape that is cherished in homes throughout Scotland.

For a few days during the competition, David Baddiel almost threatened to usurp Jimmy Hill's crown as the most despised man in the world. But he was always on a hiding to nothing. There is no-one living or dead who can irritate the Tartan Army with the ease of Jimmy Hill, a man so bereft of taste or sensitivity that he once appeared on telly wearing a bow tie fashioned from the cross of St George The most famous and tuneless song in the Tartan Army repertoire is the evergreen "We hate Jimmy Hill, he's a poof, he's a poof."

Strangely, there is little or no homophobia attached to the song. As the Scottish comedian Jerry Sadowitz once said, the word 'poof' has a totally different meaning in Scotland. It is used to describe an irritating and pestilent character, who is often conveniently English. As Sadowitz rightly explains, "Quentin Crisp is a homosexual, Jimmy Hill is a fucking poof."

Over the years, there has been a noticeable socio-economic shift in the composition of the Tartan Army. In the Seventies Scotland had an entirely male and working class following. Now there are more professional and middle class members, and significantly more women and children. This is a familiar pattern in British football in general but is perhaps more pronounced in Scotland, where following the national team has status.

Many commentators have used the shifting behaviour of the Tartan Army to gauge the political psyche of Scotland. It is a compelling if crude comparison. Basically, the theory goes like this. The emotional hype of Argentina in 1978 led to depression and disappointment. A year later the referendum on Scottish self-govern-

Special relations

The reassuring thing about being Scottish is that it gives you the right to be a two-faced hypocrite. Whenever there's a poisoned chalice waiting to be passed, you can rest assured that we want it to go to the nice guy. Take the England manager's job. Scottish football fans have a special relationship with England managers. No matter what their origins or football pedigree, we always get round to hating them sooner or later.

If I am honest, I wanted Glenn Hoddle to get the boot months before he blabbed on about reincarnation and the wheelchair brigade. He has always been too smarmy for my liking, and if it takes a bit of bogus Hindu philosophy, and a Guru in curlers to get him his P45, then that's life.

I can say without fear of contradiction that every England manager in my lifetime has been a fully-insured prat. Since devolution, many Scots feel obliged to be mature about English football. Not me – I'd rather they took the parliament back than be forced to say something nice about Kevin Keegan.

It all began with Alf Ramsey and 1966. He drove a stake through the heart of the Tartan Army by managing the England team that won the World Cup. The win itself

"If ever an England manager deserved to take a wrong turning in Possilpark it is Terry Venables"

was bad enough, but the manner of its achievement rankles even more. Alf Ramsay's side was called the 'wingless wonders'. He dispensed with the free flowing wingers of old, the flamboyant style that had characterised Scottish football for the best part of a century, preferring a more austere, tactical and probably reliable soccer system. Ramsey instinctively distrusted the Celtic nations – he would never have picked Jimmy Johnstone. As a race he considered the Scots too emotional and preferred players drained of character.

Ramsey was never slow to criticise the Scots, so I don't feel inclined to remember him fondly. Unlike his contemporary Jock Stein, Ramsey's suspicion of free expression infected his team. Outside of England they remain the most unpopular world champions ever, which is a remarkable achievement given that the Argentinean military Junta has also won the World Cup.

Terry Venables was Ramsey's polar opposite, which only goes to show that you can despise an England manager irrespective of personality. Venables is the cockney cab driver writ large, a man who has been caught on the fiddle more often than Ally Bain. He is noisy, flamboyant and full of his own self-importance: a whelk stall in the High Street of life. It doesn't seem to matter if you are on holiday in Lanzarote or in the back of a London cab, you always seem to come across a guy like Venables, mouthing off about the 'Jocks' and their Mickey Mouse money. If ever an England manager deserved to take a wrong turning in Possilpark it is Terry Venables.

Graham Taylor's departure was also a memorable experience. He seemed a decent enough bloke – so decent that he even had the foresight to make a video about his failures, a collector's item for the Tartan Army, which contains more than 70 uses of the f-word and some brilliant hang-dog expressions as England get a doing.

By 2001, Sven Goran Eriksson had become the first foreigner to hold the England job, and was greeted as a visionary appointment. But his departure from Italian club Lazio – who at the time were playing some of the most disastrous football in their history – is less well publicised. After one drubbing too many, their fans turned on the club and stoned the players' coach as it left the stadium.

As England scoured the world to get the right man, Lazio's board was divided over the most cost-effective way to sack him – a fact that has been carefully airbrushed by the media.

Eriksson's humble football origins have supposedly laid the foundations for an obsession that has taken him to the dizzy heights of world football. Humble is the operative word. Eriksson was a full-back for Karlskoga, the Forfar of Sweden, and throughout his playing days his mum never needed to stock up on the Brasso. His playing reputation was dire. I doubt if he has much to offer David Beckham when it comes to bending free kicks. Come to think of it there's not much he could tell Steven Tweed either.

The English press seized on his recently published book, which focuses on the mental capacity of footballers. The book's idea is that players fall into two distinct categories – type A players and type B players. Type A players lack the hunger to win, and type B players have a deeper passion. Eriksson claims that if you look for players who fall into the type B category there is a greater chance of winning games.

Wow! Can I try another one on you – digestive biscuits fall into two distinct categories: those with chocolate and those without. If you buy a packet with chocolate on they're a wee bit dearer than those without.

It is on the shoulders of this bewilderingly gifted genius that the future of English football rests. But to say I wish Sven-Goran Eriksson good luck would be stretching credibility. Call me a 'Type B' Scotland fan but I hope he is an abject failure.

As Jerry Sadowitz rightly explains, "Quentin Crisp is a homosexual, Jimmy Hill is a fucking poof"

ment failed and a period of anticipatory nationalism subsided. When the SNP leader Jim Sillars retired from politics he reflected back on 1978 and dismissed the Scots as "90-minute patriots."

But things have changed. The Tartan Army travels to the World Cup finals believing that the team will be knocked out. They see their role as 'pissed-up ambassadors' who simply revel in the pleasures of being there. Pragmatism has gripped their ranks. According the pundits, it shows signs of a national maturity that lay behind the faint and quiet revolution of May 1998, when the devolution referendum returned overwhelming support for a Scottish parliament.

As if to stress the symmetry of it all the first Scottish MSP to be arrested in the life of the parliament was the SNP politician Kenny McAskill – apprehended in London on his way to Scotland's Euro 2000 qualifier against England. He was exercising his constitutional right to stagger around in a kilt questioning Gary Lineker's love life.

For those who have travelled hopefully across the years, the most appealing feature of the Tartan Army lies in its ability to turn an invasion into a party.

Military jargon

Many Scots cringe when they read the military metaphors that pursue Scotland fans. The Tartan Army never arrives, instead it 'invades' cities. Its most ragged members are known as the 'foot-soldiers' and those who consume too much drink on the day of a game are often described as missing in action.

Although its members are more quaint and polite than they have been in past eras, the Tartan Army is still an awesome sight. At Italia '90, on the day of their first round match against Sweden, the Scottish fans engulfed the city of Genoa. Camped in tents and cheap hotels along the Ligurian coastline, they arrived in the city in numbers that clearly astounded local residents.

The route to Sampdoria's Luigi Ferrari Stadium was a swaying conga of over 20,000 Scots. Swedish fans either joined in or were forced to line the streets and simply applaud, as the massed pipes and drums and the drunken eightsome reels went by. Many believe that Scotland's victory was sealed in the streets outside. Although they were one of the most fancied teams in the tournament Sweden simply bottled it.

At their very best the Tartan Army belong in the elite of football fans. They are up there with the Brazilians, the Italian *Ultras*, and Barça's Catalonian battalions.

Celebrating ourselves

But by the mid-Nineties fame has gone to Scotland's head. The Tartan Army is now so accustomed to being filmed by the international media that ordinary football fans have become

Scots fans celebrate yet another World Cup disaster with customary aplomb

self-obsessed. In order to distance themselves from England fans, the Tartan Army has reinvented itself as having "the best-behaved supporters in the land". They frequently win spurious awards handed out by FIFA, although no-one has ever seen one, nor indeed has there ever been an election to decide who gets the freebie to Lake Geneva to collect the trophy.

In the era of the twee Scotland fan some are willing to go to outlandish lengths to ingratiate themselves with locals. In Mexico in 1986, Scotland fans paraded the streets of Neza, the third world Mexican township that played host to Scotland's group, giving their autographs to orphans.

Most Scotland fans have personal cuttings from the local press, where they are happy to help local journalists by lifting their kilts to reveal thistle tattoos and bare Caledonian arses.

This desire to be liked and the need to feel welcomed in a foreign city is possibly a collective response to the bad reputation of English fans. Or maybe it's just the other side of Scotland schizophrenia over-dominating the darkness.

Since football hooliganism hardened in the Eighties, the Tartan Army has perfected a form of self-policing. Fans have finely tuned antennae for what's acceptable and what is not. A safety valve controls the worst excesses of drunkenness and violence is rare.

One of the most resonant photographs of the Tartan Army in recent years was taken at a match in Stockholm. A supporter wearing a Scottish regimental hat is forcing his face through the metal grill fencing around the perimeter of the pitch. He is kissing a blonde Swedish police-woman who is clearly enjoying the liaison.

Months after the photo appeared in the press the ingratiating Scots invited her over for a holiday to show how warm a nation we are.

Sadly the woman felt coerced into accepting the invitation, came on holiday and told the Scottish press that our football fans were the best in the world.

I wish she had told us to get a life and gone to Majorca. ◊

9

THE SCOTSMAN, THE ENGLISHMAN AND THE SEX-MAD GRANNY

Erik Bo Andersen felt wetness trickle down the back of his Rangers training top – too fresh to be sweat and too heavy to a drizzle of rain. He turned to see one of the world's most famous footballers giggling with pride and wiggling a wee boy's willie inside a pair of Rangers shorts.

Andersen was a frequent victim of adolescent pranks and resigned himself to an inevitable explanation. Paul Gascoigne had pissed on his back and for the first time in the history of Hampden Babylon the word 'steaming' had a new meaning.

Gazza was at the height of his frustrating celebrity. A man-child with attention deficit disorder, whose exquisite balance and improbable range of skills had become one of the greatest players of his generation.

Alone among the group of buskers and bad boys that played with him at Ibrox, Gascoigne was capable of urinating on a fellow professional. Part of him had never graduated from a school playground in Gateshead, where his noisy talent was first noticed. England manager Bobby Robson famously dismissed him as being "daft as a brush" – here was a boy whose brains were truly in his feet.

Gascoigne's arrival at Ibrox in the summer of 1995 was like the Second Coming. Gazzamania gripped Scotland as the already paunchy English internationalist was greeted as a bleached-blond God. His transfer from Lazio for £4.3m underlined Rangers' power and wealth. It was a testament to the success of Walter Smith, who managed the club's virtual domination of Scottish football in the 1990s. But Gascoigne would never have played in Scotland had it not been for the previous Rangers manager Graeme Souness, the man who transformed the club's traditional image and, under the commercial

chairman David Murray, presided over the most significant revolution in modern Scottish football.

It is easy to imagine a Scottish international player being jailed in Barlinnie prison or a Celtic fan being shot in an Amsterdam sex bar. But try to imagine Souness and Gascoigne, one a Scot who wishes he was English, the other an Englishman whose behaviour was so inexplicably reckless he could be mistaken for a wayward Scot from the land of Hampden Babylon.

The lives and careers of Gascoigne, an unpredictable football pest, and Souness, the sober businessman, never directly intersected but they have refracted each other across two decades at many different clubs, including Tottenham, Middlesborough and, most notoriously of all, at Rangers. A passing sceptic, with a passion for national stereotypes, could be forgiven for getting their nationalities confused.

Spot the Scot? This was a confusing time for stereotypes, when the very basis of nationality itself was coming under strain. In the search for a team that could take on the world, Scottish boss Craig Brown desperately played the 'granny card', searching through the birth certificates of 'B' list English players in the hope that rogue sperm from generations ago could connect a half-decent player to the land of Caledonia. Such was Brown's desperate need for a Scottish talisman he seemed willing to scour registry offices in the Highlands hoping that a sex-mad granny had produced a promiscuous lineage that would lead inevitably to football stardom.

By 2001 the once-famous dark blue Scottish jersey, worn with intimate pride by the Wembley Wizards, had been donned by a questionable gaggle of cockneys, Brummies, and English-born Bravehearts. Brown even embarked on a flawed mission to

"Me next, me next!"

Of the seven deadly sins, only pride really matters to Graeme Souness; the other six come on as substitutes

recruit a Jamaican, the Ipswich striker David Johnson who by some vague Commonwealth compromise could play for all four home nations. It transpired that Johnson had been adopted and that in fact he was English, but the information came too late to prevent a now-familiar piece of pub trivia. Name the Scottish player whose father is Jamaican? Answer: Roy Aitken. His father's name was Jim.

The Messiah with the droop moustache

There has always been something unsettling about Graeme Souness. He's handsome – although his moustache seems to have imprisoned him

in the 1970s – and he's super-fit, despite a heart bypass. Souness is the strident enigma who spent five years dragging Glasgow Rangers into the twentieth century. The Souness revolution at Ibrox reversed the dominant trend of football transfers. Until the Eighties the traffic had been virtually one way, Scottish players lured south as part of the historic drift of football talent. But towards the end of 1988, Rangers were the subject of an inspirational takeover bid by Souness's personal friend, the businessman David Murray. The revolution cast a different future. Big-name players from England, excluded from European competition because English teams

Souness is sent off in his first game for Rangers. "I'd let my dad down, humiliated him in his own street"

were banned from participation, lived out their twilight years in Scotland picking up pay-days before the rot set in. Butcher. Roberts. Woods. Gascoigne. Every one of them was an England international capable of irritating the sensitive souls who support football teams across Scotland.

Souness first hit the headlines as a teenager when he absconded from his first club Tottenham and ran away from London to his home in Edinburgh. Homesickness, the love of a teenage girlfriend called June and a premature belief in his ability had encouraged the young Souness to jump ship.

"I was totally wrong. It was imm-ature, pure arrogance," Souness admitted, in what must be one of the few confessions to take place inside Ibrox. "I was 17 and thought I had a God-given right to be in Spurs' first team. At that time their midfield was Peters, Mullery and Perryman and I simply wasn't good enough. But I was young and Scottish and I though I was the greatest. Spurs did me a favour, I left with a chip on my shoulder and a point to prove." Gascoigne's arrival at Tottenham from Newcastle two decades later in 1988 forced the young playmaker on to a bigger stage. On his return to St James's Park to play for the London team he was pelted by his favourite food – Mars Bars.

While Gazza always tried to ingratiate himself with fans, playing to the gallery, Souness seemed to glide through games as if the fans' only role was to watch. Self-confidence border-ing on arrogance is one of Souness's most abiding characteristics. As a play-er for Middlesbrough, Liverpool and Scotland he was Renoir with a razor blade, an artistic hard man, whose flamboyant style of play was world class. When he hung on to the ball there was a strange, self-assured almost narcissistic side to his game. When Souness played, a part of him always stood aside, literally watching his own skills.

Of the seven deadly sins, only pride really matters to Graeme Souness; the other six come on as substitutes.

The chocolate soldier

Graeme Souness is always guaranteed to split public opinion. As a player for Scotland his peacock style made him a figure of considerable loathing. The diminutive midfield player Archie Gemmill once called him "the chocolate soldier", adding with barbed wit, "If Souness was chocolate he'd eat himself."

"Archie was 90 per cent right," says Souness, never slow to admit his failings. "There was a lot of truth in what he said. We are going back to 1978 – maybe I was a bit vain and thought the world revolved around me, but it was my way of motivating myself, and it worked with Archie Gemmill, every time I played him after that I kicked him up in the air."

Souness has never shrugged off his vanity. In a career that took him to Genoa where he played for Sampdoria, he assumed an almost Italianate sense of style. He was a regular in the designer bars that pose in the sun along the Portofino coastline and although he only drinks moderately, he has developed a taste for vintage champagne. He wears the kind of exaggerated Armani suits which never quite blended into the Govan landscape.

By comparison, Paul Gascoigne's arrival in Italy was bathed in brashness. The Geordie wonder-child, raised on playground pranks, had risen through the ranks of his local team, Newcastle, progressed to the club that Souness had waged war with, Spurs, and then made the meteoric leap to play in Serie A with Roman giants Lazio.

Italy had a profound and sometimes farcical effect on both men. Gazza was followed to Italy by a rag-bag of friends and hangers-on, who set up camp in his luxury villa, and turned it into the living and breathing *Viz* cartoon. Fart gags, practical jokes and fat slags fouled the air. Although he was already a millionaire, and rich beyond his own wildest imaginings, Gascoigne, for good and bad, could not quite shake off the pals he grew up with in Gateshead. First among equals was his portly best pal Jimmy 'Five Bellies' Gardner. At Lazio he offended his new hosts by belching into a news microphone. He poured oil on diplomatic waters by shouting, "Fuck off Norway"

to a TV camera, and on a corporate video he bid his guests a fond farewell with the merry words, "Happy Christmas you fucking wankers."

If Gascoigne experienced Italy as a lonely and semi-detached detour, Souness used it as a formidable entry in his professional CV. When he eventually managed Rangers, he brought the professional efficiencies of Sampdoria with him. Gascoigne held Italy at bay; Souness revelled in its reputation as the home of the greatest football league in the world. He once claimed that the drunken spirit of

ication now have primacy over wayward skills. "If you don't look after your body you have no place at this club."

Gascoigne by comparison was prone to weight gain, gorged on junk food, fought an unconvincing battle against alcohol abuse and had a peculiar habit of pissing on his team mates' backs.

"My boss is a hooligan"

Both players had highly flammable tempers but the psychology that drove them to commit indiscretions on the pitch could not be more different.

On a corporate video he bid his guests a fond farewell with the merry words, "Happy Christmas you fucking wankers"

Hampden Babylon was holding Scottish football back. "The Scottish mentality is different. In Italy they accept going into retreat during preseason training, they have strict codes on players' sex lives, it's almost religious. Scottish players simply don't understand that. I want to bring the good bits of that system to Rangers."

There is more than passing irony in the very thought of a celibate Rangers. The Italian rituro system is monastic in its rigour; players are kept away from wine, women and song for weeks on end, in order to concentrate on their game. Keeping a Rangers first team squad away from a disco would be like keeping moths from a light bulb. But Souness deplores the heritage of scandal and misbehaviours and insists that players like Baxter and Best are anachronisms. "Today the body is a footballer's only asset," he claims, adamant that fitness and ded-

When Souness lost the head, something snapped. The most chilling sight in world football is Souness sparking a near riot when he was manager of Galatasary in the notorious Turkish league. In a venomous derby match against Fenerbahce, he ran to the centre circle and using the corner flag as a spear, stabbed the flag into the ground as if medieval war had been declared.

In 1985, he claimed defensively, "There's black and white proof I'm not the killer I'm supposed to be, I've only been sent off twice." When he moved to Rangers as a player and the red cards flourished it was a quote he was destined to regret.

Jan Bartram, the Danish full-back who played for Rangers under Souness fell into disrepute at the club after a newspaper article led with the incriminating headline "My Boss Is A Hooligan". In Copenhagen's biggest-selling daily newspaper *Ekstra Bladet*,

Bartram claimed the Rangers boss had given players strict instructions to intimidate the opposition.

Bartram's dispute with Souness was the first of several highly publicised fights with players. Despite his popularity with Rangers fans, the English midfield hard man, Graham Roberts, was banished from Ibrox after a dressing room argument with Souness. To emphasise his authority the unforgiving Rangers boss exposed Roberts to a humiliating period as a reserve team substitute. The following season the wayward Derek Ferguson, elder brother of Rangers' subsequent captain Barry Ferguson, and the English international Terry Butcher also left Ibrox in a hurricane of dressing-room disagreement.

Souness believed he was a victim of a campaign bordering on conspiracy and believed that referees took an over-exuberant interest in his style of play and management. Despite the fact that he has been involved in more intimidating tackles than most professionals of his generation, Souness always argued that a line should be drawn between hard-edged professionalism and pathological violence. Not normally an apologist, he is still traumatised by the tackle, which left Hibernian's George McCluskey needing nine stitches in a knee wound. He openly admits that the foul on McCluskey was possibly the lowest moment in his career. "I've never been more depressed than the time I was sent off against Hibs. It was the first game of the season. I was brought up in Albert Street near the Hibs ground, my whole family came from that area, my dad used to sneak into the ground at night to play football on the grass at Easter Road, and I got sent off in my own backyard. I remember seeing the red card and looking up, there was 30,000 people jeering and I could see my dad in the front row of the

directors' box. I can still feel the shame now. I'd let my dad down, humiliated him in his own street. That was my lowest moment in football."

Miss world and euro disco

If Souness was good at hurting others, Paul Gascoigne had a self-destructive temper and a pernicious habit of injuring himself. When he lunged into tackles he was frequently the fall guy. In the 1991 English Cup Final he tackled Nottingham Forest's Gary Charles, damaged his cruciate ligament and missed an entire season through injury. Some say he was never as good a player when he returned. In September of the same year he

demonstrated that if his fitness was in doubt his notoriety wasn't. Gascoigne, struggling on crutches, fell down the stairs of a Newcastle nightclub prolonging what was already a serious career-threatening injury.

According to the tabloids, Souness has had remarkable success with women. By contrast, Gascoigne was a notorious failure. In the Seventies, great play was made of Souness's love affair with the former Miss World Mary Stavin and his brief flirtation with Karen Berlinski, one half of an appalling Euro disco duo who briefly graced the German hit parade. But it was his marriage to his wife Danielle, the heiress to a family fortune, which

"There's black and white proof I'm not the killer I'm supposed to be. I've only been sent off twice"

"Tell the Jock that he's freed"

finally secured the soap-opera image. Like an out-take from *Falcon Crest*, Souness and his wife moved from villa to mansion and back again, but an incurable obsession with football led to divorce and to a painful separation.

There is a more solitary side of Graeme Souness that the tabloids never readily acknowledged; obsessed with success and a wealthy victim of Scotland's passion for football.

Despite his high-profile public image as one of Scotland's most successful businessmen, Souness was a loner who never quite fitted in. He has always had a love-hate relationship with Scotland and in one infamous misquote was accused of wanting to be English. He did not hide the fact that he voted Conservative in an era when it was virtually a certifiable act

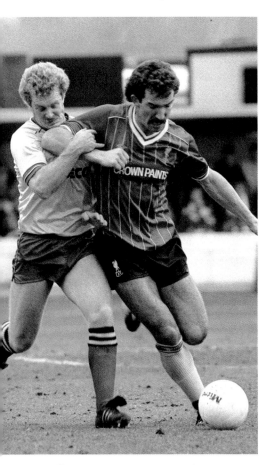

Elbow room

in Scotland. And when he returned south to manage Blackburn he pursued one of his favourite hobbies – ridding the club of its Scottish professionals; Callum Davidson, Christian Dailly and Billy McKinlay were all shown the door. Davidson once claimed that in the eyes of Souness being a Scot was a weakness.

Although he was undoubtedly one of the greatest and most committed midfield players in the history of Scottish football, Souness seems to cast doubt on his Scottishness. "I've always felt I was never popular with the Scottish crowd. I played once for Scotland against Wales and got booed every time I touched the ball. I was upset because I was proud to play for Scotland but the crowd's reaction only acted as a spur. I never backed off.

"There's a parochial side to Scotland that I've never been able to accept. When I came to Rangers I knew I'd have to change attitudes. Rangers are the biggest club in Scotland, but they had an attitude that seemed to be against change and against progress. For me it's forward or nothing and if you don't believe that you deserve to be a second-rate club or second-rate country."

His uncompromising image made him a figure of unmitigated resentment in his home country. Soon after he joined Rangers he was involved in a nasty and bitter dismissal, sacking the club's long-standing groundsman. His defenders saw it as efficiency; his detractors viewed it as the uncaring side of Graeme Souness. So desperate to be liked, Gascoigne would have cried rather than watch a grounds man walk away. He showered his money on those around him, was a soft touch for a loan and once paid £20 for a Mars Bar asking the shop assistant to give the change to local kids.

Gascoigne made millions and spent millions. Souness preferred to spend

on behalf of others, especially club chairmen. The war chest he was given at Ibrox would have been unthinkable to every previous manager. Admittedly Souness signed a few turkeys, in the uncharacteristically naïve belief that if they were English then they must be good, but in doing so he dismantled the old Ibrox Calvinism, and replaced it with a corporate entrepreneurship more finely attuned to the modern world. Rangers became a club ambitious enough to sign Paul Gascoigne.

In his first season at Ibrox, Gascoigne netted 19 times in 41 games including several goals that were of outrageous quality. It was impossible to read a tabloid paper that year that was not in some way weaving a controversial story about the peroxide Geordie.

1996 and all that

Summer 1996 was a memorable and tumultuous year in Gazza's life. It seemed as if his daft and quixotic character was unfolding in full view of an appalled and voyeuristic public.

The European Championships were to be played in England and it was a tournament that was to unfold as a drama of extreme emotions, with Scotland and England pitted against each other at Wembley in a modern re-run of the greatest show on earth.

On television the programme that seemed to have captured the *zeitgeist* of the times was Chris Evans's Friday evening chat show *TFI Friday*, a live mix of rock, comedy stunts and celebrity guests.

In the midst of it all was Paul Gascoigne, effervescent, easily led and planning to get married.

Gazza's list of misdemeanours is now legendary. He had recklessly injured himself in vital matches and shed tears for England. At Rangers he tried to endear himself to the Ibrox

Souness signed the odd turkey in the uncharacteristically naïve belief that if they were English they must be good

Souness: The moustache that Miss World fell for

faithful by playing an imaginary flute in his debut match, a friendly against Steuau Bucharest. Conned by team-mates, he naively thought the flute would be a passing gesture to the home fans. But the gesture ignited the tabloids, making Gazza Scottish football's Public Enemy Number One. Gazza was a celebrity, a demon – and a total dick. His real mistake was not religious bigotry it was naïvety and a bewildering desire to be liked, two fatal flaws that were to pursue Gascoigne throughout his Ibrox career. Seen from the vantage point of Scottish sectarianism it was an emotionally charged prank. From Gascoigne's point of view it was just a joke, the latest in a series that included arranging a date for his best pal Jimmy Five Bellies – the girl was a transvestite – booking a string of sunbed appointments for his black team mate Tony Cunningham and making fellow Geordie Chris Waddle a cappuccino made of bath foam.

By April 1996, Rangers were a single point ahead of Celtic in the Premier League title race and bitter visitors Aberdeen were heading to Ibrox in an attempt to spoil the party. A win for Walter Smith's side would secure Rangers their eighth championship in a row, agonisingly close to the 'nine in a row' record set two decades before by Celtic's Lisbon Lions. The benefits of the Souness revolution were still being reaped long after he had left the club.

In that crucial match Gascoigne demonstrated the uninhibited brilliance that set him apart from most of the players of his generation. If Souness represented a modern and ruthless efficiency, Gascoigne was a throwback to the 'tanner-ba' traditions of the past, in which a cavalier love of the ball and unpredictable feints opened up the most formidable defence.

Aberdeen opened the scoring through Brian Irvine in the nineteenth minute. But soon after Gascoigne took control of the show, collecting a Brian Laudrup corner and weaving past Dean Windass and Billy Dodds then curling a textbook goal beyond keeper Michael Watt. Suddenly the £4.3 million that Rangers had paid to attract Gascoigne back from Italy seemed loose change. With nine minutes of the match remaining Gascoigne took possession in his own half. He brushed

Picking sides

Choosing which nationality you prefer is becoming something of a fashion. But it is not a contemporary phenomenon. A recent story, tucked away on the arts pages of one of Scotland's posh newspapers, exposed the fact that one of our most inspired poets William McGonagall was in fact Irish.

Not since the Wigan and former Motherwell midfielder Ged Brannan attempted to turn his back on his native England to join the Cayman Islands has a nation had greatness so cruelly plucked from its midst.

> **Imagine the poetic genius paying a tribute to the Rangers coaching system in an 'Ode to Bert van Lingen'**

I'm sure there are literary theorists who will argue that Burns, Shakespeare, Wordsworth and Keats are greater poets. But for those of us who believe that any half-decent poem has to rhyme, then there is only one master: William Topaz McGonagall.

Few would not be moved by McGonagall's tribute to Tannadice – "The Tay, the Tay the silvery Tay it flows frae Perth tae Dundee, aw day." Or indeed his ode to the Scottish national football team, after another famous London victory: "Doon the line the train came puffin. Scotland two England nuthin."

McGonagall's loss to Scotland ranks alongside Tommy Coyne's caps for the Irish Republic as one of the great travesties of modern time. According to local historians, extant records of a census on local families in Dundee prove that McGonagall was born in Ireland and moved to the City of Jute, Jam and Jakeys as an infant.

To escape the discrimination often shown against the Irish in the 19th century, he or his family faked the certificates to secure McGonagall's Scots heritage. So in fact one of Caledonia's greatest literary figures was an impostor.

McGonagall leaves behind a legacy of inspired doggerel. Words are tortured into shape. Emotions are scattered to the wind. And everyday sentiments are given poetic charm. Nothing matters to McGonagall except that they rhyme. He is poetry's answer to a dour centre-half: forget the finery just boot a metaphor into the stand.

But we can only guess what the Bard of Dundee would have made of today's football. The influx of foreign players would have been a nightmare for McGonagall. Celtic's Joos Valgaeren or Rangers' Peter Lovenkrands do not exactly lend themselves to brilliant rhymes.

Mind you, some of Scottish football's foreign legion is tailor-made for McGonagall. His use of Scottish doggerel and everyday speech would have been suited to some names. Imagine the poetic genius paying tribute to the Rangers coaching system in an *Ode to Bert Van Lingen*. The words *clingin*, *mingin* and *hingin* would have dripped effortlessly from the bard's quill.

Surely the great rhymer would have penned a lustful sonnet to Craig Brown's record collection and his love of Nat King Cole. Or a personal tribute to Dick Advocaat's tactical skills, comparing him to an old Dutch Master. But alas the bard would be stumped by television commentators – even Scotland's greatest poet would struggle to find a word that rhymes with Jim Delahunt.

aside the entire Aberdeen midfield and bearing down on goal drove a left-foot shot past the Aberdeen 'keeper. It was a wonder goal and it effectively crowned Gascoigne as Scotland's footballer of the year. In a more unsettling sense it also acted as a prescient warning to Scotland. Gascoigne, now resident in Renfrewshire, and one of Scotland's most notorious citizens, would be wearing an England jersey when the world's oldest football enemies met at Wembley.

In the run up to Euro '96 it was as if Paul Gascoigne had beguiled the press. They became obsessed with his life, pursuing every strange turn and pouncing on any perceived misdemeanour.

Gascoigne for his part was a willing accomplice. He went on a highly publicised and debauched bender with the *TFI Friday* presenter Chris Evans and his side-kick Danny Baker. He played cabaret piano at the Duck Bay Marina in the company of the pop star Robbie Williams and Rangers midfielder Jorg Albertz, a heavy-smoking German with a distinct Scottish accent. He travelled with England to the Far East on a warm-up tour prior to the tournament and appeared on the front pages when he celebrated his birthday, with a group of England players. In a bar ritual, killer cocktails were poured down Gazza's throat as he was strapped into a dentist's chair. Gazza then upset passengers on a Cathay Pacific flight home. According to the England player Stuart Pearce, the captain threatened to throw Gazza off the plane and leave him stranded in Russia.

In June 1996 Gascoigne married his girlfriend Sheryl at a garish and flamboyant society wedding. She wore virginal white with a tight-cupped top barely securing her ample breasts. Gazza had parked his trademark false plastic tits for the day, in favour of a white regency coat and bright peroxide hair.

Within four months the marriage was in trouble, after Gascoigne beat his wife, injuring her face and arm in a luxury suite at the Gleneagles Hotel. After 785 days of marital bliss, Senior District Judge Gerald Angel at the Principal Registry of the Family Division in Central London granted a divorce decree in only two minutes.

In a more touching moment it was revealed that Gascoigne liked to escape

the game swung England's way. Gascoigne picked up the ball, darted towards the Scottish goal, chipped the ball over the head of Colin Hendry and bore down on Andy Goram's goal.

Here was a moment of immense drama and significance. Two Rangers team mates faced each other playing for opposing countries. Goram had been born in England the son of a Scottish footballer, and had returned 'home' from Oldham to play for Hibs, Rangers and Scotland. For Gascoigne,

There was a dick at Ibrox before Advocaat: Gascoigne plays the pie-eyed piper

Gascoigne in his bizarre and touching way liked to boast he was a Scottish international

the media attention and fish on the lochs and rivers of his beloved Scotland. In fact he even represented a Renfrewshire village in a British village fishing competition, and thus in his own bizarre and touching way liked to boast that he was a Scottish international. As Souness sought to be English a piece of Paul Gascoigne's fragmenting heart was at home with Scotland and the Ibrox dressing room bad-boys who had taken him to their heart.

Gascoigne arrived at Wembley drunk on over-exposure; Scotland had come via Villa Park, where they secured a draw in their opening game against Holland. Ironically, Scotland, who had been the first team out of the draw, were pronounced the home team at Wembley. The game is now etched in the traumatised memory of all Scottish football fans. After losing a goal to England's Alan Shearer, Scotland won a penalty, taken by Gary McAllister. Some say the ball moved. The psycho-guru Uri Geller claims he used psychic powers to trick Scotland. Whatever happened Seaman saved and

Scotland was his adopted home and the place he had said that he would one day retire. His pal Jimmy 'Five Bellies' described a man that seemed by some strange osmosis to be turning into a Scot. "He spends £100 in the fruit machine at his local pub. He is happy to sit there until he is thrown out."

Goram remembers the pub bore's greatest moment with haunting precision. "I went out so sure that he would hit the ball to the near post as I had seen him do so often in the past. But of course he let me commit myself before sending it beyond me. I knew it was a goal. I knew without looking and I remember thinking, Not him, not Gazza, because I knew he would give me stick and I wasn't sure I could take it on this occasion."

Gazza ran on beyond the net and collapsed on his back milking the goal. His victorious English team mates crowded around him. By chance a bottle of re-hydrating liquids was lying on the grass, and in a scene which seemed to parody the infamous dentist's chair in the Hong Kong cocktail bar, English

players squirted liquid into Gazza's delighted mouth.

It is a scene that drives a stake through the heart of Scottish football. Not only was it a glorious and impetuous goal, it was scored at Wembley by a wayward and flawed genius, on the ground that Scottish legends had once terrorised. It was a goal that Jim Baxter could have scored but didn't. It was a goal Hughie Gallacher could have scored but didn't. It was a goal Ally McCoist could have scored but didn't.

It was scored by an Englishman, whose drunken and violent behaviour was trapped in a body born to play football.

Paul Gascoigne's story has a peculiarly dark and Scottish logic. No wonder Graeme Souness looked to his heart and felt English. ◊

10

A VOLCANO ERUPTS AT CELTIC PARK

It was 1994 and Fabio Capello, the boss of European Cup champions AC Milan, had a problem. He had taken the world's most successful club side on a tour of the Far East, culminating in an exhibition match in China.

Capello's Milan had just won the Italian *Scudetto* for the fourth time in five years and he was universally recognised as the best manager in the world. In fact he had already agreed to join Spanish super-club Real Madrid as manager. But, at the height of his power, he had a worry.

Capello was beginning to suspect that the tricky striker he had signed from Napoli was not playing to his full potential. He knew the player was prone to erratic behaviour and could explode like a grenade, but he felt that the Beijing exhibition crowd deserved more from the lacklustre stars who were playing up front for Milan.

Baggio was doing nothing. Lentini looked uninterested. And in the words of Scottish managers he had met at UEFA coaching academies, "the wee man was taking the piss".

He decided to substitute Paolo Di Canio.

It was like a red rag to a bull, a naked flame at a petrol station or a bacon roll at a Barmitzvah. Di Canio made his way to Milan's technical area, his hands held out in comic disbelief and, like a roman candle, his combustible temper ignited.

"You're crazy. You're sick in the head," Di Canio screamed. In full view of the bewildered Chinese spectators, Capello lunged at Di Canio, punches were thrown, threats were exchanged and disgrace unfolded. Milan's coaching staff were momentarily stunned by the vitriol and had to rush from the bench to separate the manger and his volcanic striker.

"Fuck off to Madrid," Di Canio

shouted, as the fight was pursued up the tunnel. By now at the end of his much longer emotional fuse, Capello retaliated with one of the great put downs in the history of football.

"I'll fuck off to Madrid, if you fuck off to Scotland."

And you know what? Di Canio did.

Star Paolo di Canio's agent Moreno Roggi was already deep in negotiations with Celtic, who were anxious to find a charismatic talisman to bring success to a failing club. When he returned home from the Far East, refusing to even acknowledge Capello on the long flight back to Italy, Di Canio broke the news to his wife. They were moving to Glasgow.

Betta Di Canio, Paolo's long-suffering wife, had never heard of the place. So the couple huddled round the kitchen table with a map of Europe trying to find Glasgow. Eventually a nervous finger pointed to the map.

There it was. Just south of Iceland, not far from Clydebank.

Meet the mean streets

When Di Canio first arrived in Glasgow, the city made a murky impression on him. In his self-aggrandising autobiography, where he blames the world and his brother for a tempestuous career, he described Glasgow in unflattering terms. "It was cold and rainy, the streets were empty," Di Canio wrote. "It looked almost post-nuclear."

When Di Canio arrived at his first day of training it must have registered just how humiliating his transfer really was. Celtic had once been a force in Europe but long before Di Canio had kicked a ball. At Milan he had shared a dressing room with Franco Baresi, Roberto Donadoni, Mauro Tassotti, Roberto Baggio and Gigi Lentini. Waiting to greet him at Parkhead was a Coatbridge legend Peter Grant.

Celtic had not convincingly recovered from the sustained traumas of the early Nineties, when the club faced bankruptcy and fans went to war with the club's old and infirm board.

The legacy of a 'biscuit-tin' mentality had yet to be purged from the club. It was seen as miserly, economically challenged and struggling to catch up with Rangers, bitter and better funded rivals across the city.

Too much expectation had been placed on the shoulders of players who had come from the west of Scotland's Catholic families. Paul McStay, the recently departed captain, remained devoted to the club against his better interests and retired early due to injury never playing for another club. Peter Grant, a diehard Celtic fan from Coatbridge who briefly became Di Canio's roommate, considered himself a fan on the pitch.

Even club boss Tommy Burns, who

"I Never lick ass, Meester McCann"

At Milan he had shared a dressing room with Franco Baresi, Roberto Baggio and Gigi Lentini. Waiting to greet him at Parkhead was Coatbridge legend Peter Grant

signed Di Canio, had been born and raised a few miles from the ground and saw his love for Celtic inextricably bound up in his devotion to the Catholic faith.

For many years Celtic were characterised by under-achievement and incompetence, lurching from one self-imposed crisis to another. For a long period in the early 1990s, the club had seriously considered moving from their spiritual home in the East End of Glasgow to a toxic waste site in Cambuslang, where the old board imagined that a super new suburban stadium could be built.

Frustrated by serial failure and poor financial management, rebel fans organised against the club. Over a period of years they managed to amass enough support to become a serious threat to the family dynasties – the Whites and the Kellys – that had controlled the club for most of its history.

The rebel fans gathered shares, by tracking down the diaspora of Celtic fans scattered around the world, and a momentum gathered around an unlikely saviour, Fergus McCann, a Canadian entrepreneur who had once been the treasurer of a Celtic supporters' club in Croy.

McCann looked like the gnomic schoolteacher from the cartoon series South Park and spoke with a beguiling transatlantic drawl. He was a successful businessman who had made his millions in sports travel but was far from flamboyant. His hat of choice was the old bunnet of his Lanarkshire working class origins rather than a fedora or a homburg.

Celtic at death's door

In the early months of 1994 Celtic stared bankruptcy in the face. Debts were mounting and the Bank of Scotland was beginning to think the unthinkable. Only hours before the plugs were pulled on one of Scotland's biggest clubs, McCann came to the rescue. As rain poured down on his old man's hat, and water ran down his nose, McCann told the small band of Celtic rebels and scrum of radio and TV journalists that the battle was over; the rebels had taken control of the club.

McCann began the tough job of reversing Celtic's fortunes. Neither he nor his supporters could have predicted just how successful his rebuilding campaign would become nor indeed that he would end up in an acrimonious legal dispute about the word 'promise' and the way it would be interpreted by Paolo Di Canio.

Seven years after he took control of Celtic, Parkhead had been refurbished and was now Scotland's biggest sports stadium, Rangers' runaway success had been halted, and a new optimism gripped Celtic Park.

"I might have trouble fitting this shirt over my head"

McCann retired just as he said he would and moved to the Caribbean, with his wife Elspeth and their newly-born children, believing that his relationship with Celtic was over.

Di Canio had moved on like a fitful mercenary, first to Sheffield Wednesday then to West Ham. In September 1998 during a league match against Arsenal he infamously pushed the match referee Paul Alcock.

In his fertile mind, Paolo Di Canio was always misunderstood and badly done by. This time he believed he had been singled out by the referee, and then misrepresented as a violent player. But his act of contrition was reluctant for a man born and raised near the Vatican. "Believe me," he wrote a few years later, "if I wanted to do something violent, it would have been totally different."

The notoriety he attracted in England's Premiership brought book publishers to his door, and in 2000 Harper Collins paid Paolo to publish his autobiography.

The book was printed in Glasgow and its ramifications were to revive his feud with Fergus McCann.

Di Canio used his autobiography as therapy. He sought revenge on his tormentors. He rubbished his old boss Capello, questioned the parentage of the Rangers midfielder Ian Ferguson, and blamed Fergus McCann for his decision to leave his 'beloved' Celtic.

McCann must have choked on his Pina Colada. At was as if Di Canio was haunting his retirement. He instructed his lawyers to pursue the Italian for libel, and so the two men who best symbolised the re-birth of Glasgow Celtic were to meet again, this time in court.

Curse of negative energy

The personal animosity between Fergus McCann and Paolo Di Canio seemed to crystallise the intrigue, dis-

"I take it there's a fee?"

putes and internal wrangling that had blighted Celtic for decades. Not since the halcyon days of Jock Stein and Jimmy Johnstone in the late Sixties had censorious management and a volatile ball-playing winger come into such dramatic conflict.

Yet again the words 'Celtic' and 'turmoil' met in the same sentence.

To understand the level of animosity that had grown up between McCann and Di Canio, you have to begin with their diametrically opposed personalities. Di Canio was mercurial and creative, McCann was driven and old-fashioned.

The controversial General Manager of Celtic, Jock Brown, who presided over one of the club's stormiest periods between June 1997 and November 1998 provided the perfect pen-portrait of McCann.

"He is razor-sharp mentally," Brown said "Totally focused, utterly determined and wouldn't know how to

ingratiate himself with anyone. He calls a spade a spade and can be immensely impatient and frequently intolerant, he certainly doesn't suffer fools gladly nor is he too adept at trying to spare people's feelings."

Come to think of it McCann sounds quite like Paolo Di Canio.

And maybe that was the problem. Far from being polar opposites, a dogged individualism united both of them. At times they seemed like they were actually the same man in outlandishly different bodies. Scottish football's first multiple personality disorder had checked into the sanatorium at Parkhead.

Paolo Di Canio grew up in Rome's Quarticciolo district – a bit like Springburn but closer to monuments – and first rose to fame in Italy when he appeared as Zorro on an Italian amateur TV show. He signed for local club Lazio as a teenager, rose through the youth ranks and in 1986 won the Italian youth title with Lazio in Cesena's Stadio Olimpico before moving to Serie C2 team Ternana.

During his medical for Italian military service Di Canio discovered he had a serious leg injury which had thus far been treated by cortisone injections. Under the threat of amputation, he went to a series of specialists in Italy, but his conditions worsened with panic attacks, dizziness and uncontrollable bursts of emotion.

Eventually Di Canio was talked into visiting a faith healer in the rambling hills outside Terni. The faith healer made a remarkable diagnosis that Fergus McCann would have eagerly approved of:

"Paolo," she said, "there's nothing wrong with you, you are just filled with negative energy."

But he was not alone. Di Canio's brief and belligerent period in Scottish football broadly coincided with the presence of two other Celtic strikers, who together would have tested the patience of Job, let alone the easily irritated McCann.

One man, one contract

Pierre van Hooijdonk, a Dutch striker signed from FC Breda, was the SPL's top striker in season 1995–6, scoring 26 goals and leaving the Rangers trio Ally McCoist, Gordon Durie and Paul Gascoigne in his wake.

But statistics tell only half the story. Van Hooijdonk was an enigma. He was a strong and magisterial presence up front at a time when Celtic fans longed for a hero, but behind the scenes, in the dressing room and in the interminable meetings with his agent, he was a sullen, evasive and unreliable character.

Van Hooijdonk embodied the frustrating extremes of Dutch football. He was an immensely skilled player for his size, technically sophisticated and hugely athletic, but he was also staggeringly arrogant and capable of unbelievable contempt for those around him.

Van Hooijdonk had been reared on the dressing room dissent that blights Dutch football, and pursued a strange existentialism that only he can explain.

At Celtic, he replaced the old philosophical motto – I think therefore I am – with a personal belief system more attuned to the philosophical certainties of the modern footballer: I am in a contract dispute therefore I am.

When he eventually left Celtic to join Nottingham Forest it was not long before his personality upset his new club. After some outstanding performances – yet again as top scorer – he walked out on Forest claiming that his team mates simply weren't good enough and that the club lacked ambition. Van Hooijdonk passed through the excess baggage gate, checked his ego in at Heathrow and

Life without Celtic

Just imagine that Celtic didn't exist. What would Scottish football be like? Would it be a richer or a poorer place? Some insight can be gained by looking across the water to Ireland. In 1947, the country's most successful football club was virtually written out of history. After a fractious Boxing Day derby against Linfield, Belfast Celtic simply disappeared.

In the bad old days when sectarianism was rife in Scotland, it was conceivable that events off the pitch could have led to the demise of Glasgow Celtic. But someone up there smiled on Jock Stein and placed a lasting curse on Belfast Celtic.

The events of Ireland's Boxing Day massacre are now part of sectarian legend. At the time, Belfast Celtic were the form team in the Irish League, on a 31-game unbeaten run when they met arch-rivals Linfield at Windsor Park, in a match trailed very much like an Old Firm derby, as a psychological thriller that would decide the destiny of the League title.

According to eyewitnesses it was the most bitter and badly behaved match in modern football. The match ended in a draw, but as the riot police descended on the ground, Belfast Celtic's star player Jimmy Jones was dragged into the crowd and kicked senseless.

> **According to eyewitnesses it was the most bitter and badly behaved match in modern football**

It was not the first time that Linfield and Belfast Celtic had clashed. In 1912, 100 people were injured at one match – four by gunshot – when a riot broke out at half-time. When Belfast Celtic left the Irish League its fan base naturally looked across the water to their natural allies in Glasgow. To this day, Celtic's Northern Ireland support has nostalgia for the club that disappeared.

In every key respect Belfast Celtic was the Irish answer to Martin O'Neill's team: they played in green and white hoops, their ground was nicknamed Paradise and they flew the flag for the city's poorest citizens. There was, of course, one key difference. Harald Brattback would never have got a game for Belfast Celtic.

The demise of Belfast Celtic is a sad chapter in the blighted history of football in Northern Ireland. For fans in Scotland, we can use the club as a reminder of how far Scottish football has travelled to remove the corrosive influence of religious bigotry from our game. Everyone knows that there are still out there whose minds stopped evolving in 1690 and there are others who cannot see an offside flag without imagining a grand Masonic conspiracy. But the vast majority of Scottish football fans have managed to get sectarianism into perspective: it is like scurvy – a pathetic relic of some bygone era.

The influx of foreign players has had a catalytic effect. The Italian imports at Ibrox have underlined the fading ludicrousness of being a 'Protestant' team on the eve of a European super-league. There has been the odd reported singing of *The Sash* by the Rangers squad in past years, but I cannot think of many players who would be remotely interested in the song or its sentiments.

When Rangers signed Neil McCann – reputedly the first Scottish Catholic at the club since the days of Mo Johnston – what was remarkable was that no-one seemed to care. No doubt there was someone out there threatening to burn his season ticket. But no-one was listening. Celtic have embraced the future too: Fergus McCann transformed Celtic into a modern and commercially viable club.

So there but for the grace of history goes Scotland. When Belfast Celtic disbanded, they left a vacuum in Irish league football that has never been filled. Most Belfast fans would argue that their disappearance has taken a competitive edge out of football in the city, and left Northern Ireland with a soccer culture that is at best semi-professional.

Without Celtic Scotland's record in international club football would be impoverished. No Celtic, no Lisbon Lions and no European Cup in 1967.

But every cloud has a silver lining. No Celtic, no Andy Payton and no Carl Muggleton. And just think we would have been spared the mind-numbing boredom of the Mark Viduka saga; his long-winded transfer to Leeds was a series of unfolding events that would drive a sane man to Tempazepam.

It seems unimaginable now, but there was a time in Scottish football when Celtic didn't exist. The club, founded in 1888, is a comparatively late entrant to the game. Kilmarnock were founded 19 years before anyone had ever heard of Celtic. I wonder if there's an old-timer down in Ayrshire who remembers the good old days.

No hit-men in pubs in Holland, no restricted-view seats, and no songs about the shortage of potatoes.

"You can," Bassett said, like an Israeli leader in search of peace, "stick it up your arse"

headed back to Holland.

Van Hooijdonk's disappearance from Forest was driven by some of his personality traits already demonstrated at Parkhead. He threatened to retire, refused to return and sulked in a style that would have shamed a spoilt child. Eventually he was provoked by his contract into returning, but only for a brief and uncomfortable stay. When he returned to Nottingham he claimed he wanted to offer his boss Dave Bassett an olive branch. "You can," Bassett said, like an Israeli leader in search of peace, "stick it up your arse." Shunned by most of the team mates he had undermined and now distrusted by the fans, it was inevitable he would leave Forest.

Van Hooijdonk and Di Canio would have tried the tolerance of most managers. But their idiosyncrasies were not complete without the behavioural disorders of a third, arguably even more enigmatic, striker the Portuguese internationalist Jorge Cadete.

On the surface Cadete was by far the most reasonable of Celtic's three busketeers but beneath his long curly hair lay a mind of deep complexity.

Cadete had haunted Scottish football long before his arrival at Parkhead. In 1993, in Lisbon's Stadium of Light, he humiliated pedestrian Scotland defender Richard Gough as Andy Roxburgh's side conceded five goals.

It was, according to the dramatic hubris of Scottish football, "the night a team died". For what seemed like the longest 90 minutes in the history of Scottish football, Cadete led a wave of raids on a Scottish defence that simply wilted in his presence.

Rent boys and rumours

The night a team died was to provide a curious postscript several years later, when Richard Gough published his autobiography. To hype the book in papers, he claimed that Scotland's tactics on the night were fashioned by a Portuguese taxi driver and that Craig Brown, then Roxburgh's assistant, had based the game plan on a casual conversation in a Lisbon cab.

Such was the storm, that Scottish journalists scoured Lisbon looking for the cab driver, blaming him and not Scotland's shell-shocked defence for the travesty at the Stadium of Light.

Angered by the criticism, Andy Roxburgh and Craig Brown, who prided themselves in being kings of pre-match preparation and doyens of the dossier, retaliated. With Gough's criticisms dominating the back pages, Roxburgh told the press that he had stories that would put the former Scotland captain on the front pages. Coincidentally, a Scottish Premier League player had been arrested in Glasgow for consorting with gay rent boys. The culprit was the tragically deceased Hearts striker Justin Fashanu, but for the few days in which his identity was a mystery, a baseless rumour gripped Scotland. Fans put two and two together and got an urban legend. To this day variations of the legend crop up wherever football fans meet.

Jorge Cadete's hat trick against Scotland heightened expectations when he arrived at Celtic in 1996. Although Celtic were enduring a seemingly endless phase of rebuilding, they were beginning to amass a formidable attacking force – Di Canio, Van Hooijdonk, Cadete and the former East German internationalist Andreas Thom.

For all his swashbuckling speed and gregarious goal-scoring Jorge Cadete was a loner. In many respects he was ill-suited to football and certainly unprepared for the intrusiveness and high visibility that greets players when they sign for either side of the Old Firm.

Unlike Di Canio, who was so obsessed with his personal development that he would train alone for long periods perfecting ball tricks, Cadete preferred to be on his own. In contrast to Van Hooijdonk, who seemed to glide above his teammates presuming he was their better, Cadete seemed to need to be alone.

By the time Cadete returned to Lisbon for a summer break at the end of the 1996–7 season he was hugely popular with the Celtic support. Despite some strange and distant behaviour and a bizarre series of episodes in which he worried about the welfare of his pet dog, it was presumed that Jorge would return.

But when he failed to report for pre-season training, the club suspected that another PR disaster was staring them in the face. The club requested medical certificates to explain Cadete's absence and they duly arrived from Cadete's agent. Although the full detail of the certificates have never been released, they intimated that Cadete was suffering from depressive illness and was experiencing psychological difficulties.

The press had a field day. Cadete was stereotyped as a football flake lying on a Freudian couch awaiting psycho-analysis. Cynics suggested he should cut off his trademark curls to take the

Cadete was stereotyped as a flake … cynics suggested he should cut off his trademark curls to take the weight off his aching head

Freud's favourite player was nuts about Celtic

Mount Etna finally meets his match

"I don't think I have ever been so angry in my life. Ever. There is no question in my mind that I would have hurt him severely"

weight of his aching head. Tired of the antics of well-paid players, many Celtic fans simply thought Cadete was contriving his illness. In the words of the perennial pub know-all, he was 'at it'.

As the season ahead loomed, General Manager Jock Brown was dispatched to Lisbon to talk Cadete into returning. It was a doomed mission. Cadete had moved to Celtic without his domineering wife and beloved dogs. Although he had been engulfed by fan worship and scored with ease, he never settled in the nomadic and isolated life of hotel rooms and room service that Celtic had generously provided.

It's a wonderful life

Jock Brown describes Cadete's domestic life as eerily comfortable. "There was an orchard in the garden and a swimming pool," he observed. "Dog kennels provided better accommodation than many people occupying the inner city of Lisbon… The house itself was immaculate… But not much else about Jorge's life appeared to be fun."

Celtic's medical team were keen to examine Cadete, believing he was in fact an able and willing employee who was seriously suffering. Celtic's Dr Jack Mulhearn had also travelled to Lisbon to talk to Cadete. His professional view was that the striker was indeed experi-

encing psychological problems and needed treatment.

Celtic tried to convince Cadete to return to Glasgow but his reluctant and influential wife refused to contemplate moving, and balked at the thought of their beloved dogs going into quarantine.

Within a matter of a few weeks Cadete was sold at a discounted price to Celta Vigo, within commuting distance of Jorge's home. The medical certificates had made Cadete a greater risk for a buying club, and Celtic never realised the money they should have received for a striker at the very height of his career.

To this day Jorge Cadete's psychological condition remains confusing and unresolved. Some fans claim he was a malingerer, others that he was simply homesick, but the likelihood exists that Jorge Cadete was suffering from a debilitating depressive illness, darker and more pitiful than the cruel generalisations of football fans will ever permit.

The volcano erupts

Paolo Di Canio was easier to fathom. He was volcanic, a product of the Stromboli School of football, with a temperament that frequently poured molten emotional lava.

Mount Etna might have only simmered on Sunday 16th March 1997 but Di Canio positively erupted.

Celtic had one last chance to stop Rangers clinching their ninth championship in a row, equalling the nine-in-a-row record that the Lisbon Lions had set in 1975. Rangers had won the previous three Old Firm derbies, and injuries had forced manager Walter Smith to increase the temperature, by hurriedly bringing the towering Mark Hateley back to Glasgow for a second spell at the club.

Hateley had been the scourge of Celtic for several years and his presence alone was intimidating.

"I always kick ass, Mr Di Canio"

Notorious for his brightly coloured and ill-considered Versace clothes, he was as famed throughout Scotland for his terrible taste in shirts as he was for his powerful forward play. Arriving at Glasgow Airport the day before the game, one joke of the time reported it was the first time Glasgow Airport's baggage staff had put a shirt *back* into a bag.

Celtic's preparation had not been perfect either; the week before Van Hooijdonk had been sold after an acrimonious contract dispute. Di Canio and Cadete were to be played together up front.

Rangers were five points ahead in the League. Celtic had run out of options: a win was vital. The only goal came late in the first half: Ian Durrant crossed into the box and the Great Dane Brian Laudrup bundled the ball into Celtic's net. Celtic were facing defeat and the real fun was about to begin.

In the second half Hateley was red-carded after an incident with the rugged Celtic stopper Malky Mackay. The game deteriorated into a vindictive and bad-tempered battle. Rangers midfielder Ian Ferguson, a Rangers fan from Glasgow's East End, was picking off the Celtic team with tough and sometimes reckless tackles.

Di Canio was losing his grip on reality. As the final whistle blew he sank to his knees in melodramatic grief. The Rangers team celebrated with their fans goading the home support with the premature and ultimately baseless chant, "Ten in a Row – Hello Hello."

It was obvious that Di Canio and Ferguson would clash and the inevitable happened. As the two players provoked each other, Di Canio claims that Ferguson called him a "bastard". Ferguson for his part refuses to be drawn into a dispute with the unpredictable Italian. Di Canio alone bears witness to a strange, almost deranged, incident:

"We had just lost the game and the title in front of our own fans at Celtic Park, our temple, and this guy Ian Ferguson, this nobody, had the gall to come up to me and insult me for no reason.

"I was not going to stand for that. I turned and chased him across the pitch. He had run over to where his team mates were celebrating. But I wasn't going to let him get away. It was obvious he was terrified. I grabbed him but the struggle didn't last long. Other players swarmed in to separate us.

"It's a good thing they did. I would have beaten him to a pulp. I don't think I have ever been so angry in my life. Ever. There is no question in my mind that I would have hurt him severely."

Di Canio played at a time in Celtic's history when delusions were rife and with the benefit of hindsight we can only marvel at his self-belief that the diminutive Italian would have beaten a hard-bitten Glasgow street-fighter to a pulp. Even the Mafia would have not welcomed a 'square go' with some of Ian Ferguson's mates.

With Van Hooijdonk gone and the title lost, manager Tommy Burns was sacked. It was only a matter of time before Di Canio and Cadete would move too.

Trading Places

Paolo Di Canio's departure at Celtic Park provoked a controversy over a single word – promise. He claims that he was given a gentleman's agreement – a promise – that if he was successful at Celtic his contract would be improved. There was no doubt that Di Canio was successful: despite his temperament he easily won the Players'

Celtic were blazing a trail for the next generation of scandal – foreign chicanery, contractual disputes and egotistical personalities

Player of the Year Award, beating the formidable Brian Laudrup.

McCann and everyone associated with Celtic deny the promise ever took place and it remains a matter of dispute.

When Di Canio left to join Sheffield Wednesday another very different word marked the controversy. For weeks prior to his departure Celtic were trying to hold on to the popular Italian. New manager Wim Jansen had identified two players he wanted to recruit and both had Dutch connections: the black striker Regi Blinker who had won under-21 caps for Holland and Henrik Larsson, a Swede who was playing at Jansen's former club Feyernoord.

Jansen's arrival coincided with the controversial and unpopular decision to recruit the lawyer and former sports commentator Jock Brown as General Manager. The press mobilised against Brown and pursued his every decision with voracious spite.

As he tried vainly to keep Di Canio at the club and go about the business of recruiting Blinker and Larsson, the press pursued hourly updates always asking the same question: would Di Canio be sold? Brown denied that was his intention and when the Italian moved to Sheffield told the press he had not been sold but "traded". It was a fine distinction that did not endear Brown to the press and meant that the

likeable Blinker's arrival was clouded in bad feeling.

To be fair to Brown – not words that you will have read much before – he did preside over the signature of two subsequent Celtic legends: Henrik Larsson and Lubo Moravcik. Both were greeted with caustic suspicion when they arrived and it was only long after Brown had gone that their true worth was spectacularly revealed.

Regi had mixed success at Celtic Park but did achieve one footnote in scandal when he was arrested in Glasgow for peeing up a back alley. This anticipated a much more infamous incident at the end of the 2001 season, when three Celtic players from the club's victorious treble side were accused of urinating in the corridors of a city centre hotel. The players had congregated to celebrate an outstanding season under new boss Martin O'Neill, in which a striker broke almost every existing record in Scottish football. His name of course was Henrik Larsson.

The coincidences that brought Paolo Di Canio, Pierre van Hooijdonk and Jorge Cadete together in the same Celtic team characterise the changes that football in Scotland was experiencing in the mid 1990s.

The Bosman ruling had opened the door to shorter contracts and the free movement of footballers across Europe. Cultural misunderstandings

were commonplace, agents were a necessary evil and the economics of football had been revolutionised.

The revolution will be televised

Although Celtic had been founded as a charity, to help the Catholic poor, Fergus McCann had overseen their transformation into a successful plc. The Scottish League had meanwhile been transformed into the more entrepreneurial SPL, an elite of clubs with their own all-seater stadiums. The cult of celebrity had set players further apart from the mass of fans and the rise of player-power meant that there was no longer the realistic prospect of footballers staying at one club for much more than a couple of years.

Even scandal was changing. Rangers, fortified by Paul Gascoigne and Andy Goram, were doing their best to keep the old traditions of drunken binges, pub fights and sex scandals in the headlines, but Celtic were blazing a trail for the next generation of scandal – foreign chicanery, contractual disputes and egotistical personalities.

As Fergus McCann enjoyed his retirement far away in the West Indies, he imagined that the bizarre challenge of rebuilding Celtic was behind him, but the memory of three professional footballers had not yet been purged from his mind. Anger had been bottled up inside him for years now.

One person in particular irritated him to the point of exasperation and neither the Caribbean sun nor a Banana Daiquiri could calm him down. Fergus had one lasting tribute to pay to Paolo Di Canio and his mates. And when it came it was classic Fergus McCann. The man in the checked bunnet, who by his dogged determination had rescued Celtic from extinction, had lost none of his rapier skills.

Rangers, fortified by Paul Gascoigne and Andy Goram, were doing their best to keep the traditions of drunken binges, pub fights and sex scandals in the headlines

"What do you mean you're not sending me off?"

A message to you, Paulo

McCann sent his best wishes back to Glasgow from his luxury retirement home, to communicate his respect for the Celtic captain Tom Boyd, who was celebrating his testimonial year.

Boyd had won the Scottish Cup with his home-town team Motherwell in 1991, moved to Celtic in their troubled years and gone on to win more than 50 caps for Scotland. But perhaps the most trying role he ever took on was the shop steward or players' representative during the frustrating years when Di Canio, Van Hooijdonk and Cadete were at the club.

Disputes about contracts, bonuses and even charity appearances seemed to be a weekly occurrence and Boyd negotiated his way though the turmoil with dignity and determination. There must have been times when strangling his team mates would have seemed reasonable.

Fergus McCann certainly thought so. On the eve of Boyd's testimonial against Manchester United he paid his own unique tribute:

"Tom Boyd captained the team in a way that commands our respect and admiration… during a period when the dressing room has had its fair share of egocentric under-achievers, med-iocre moaners and greedy rascals manipulating the media and emotions of the fans for their own ends."

It is a towering and unforgiving tribute to the real story of Celtic FC, in an era when players kissed the badge for their own self-centred ends. ◊

11
A BITTER PILL
TO SWALLOW

Mrs Margaret Johnston, a 32-year-old housewife living in Sutton Coldfield, came on like a country and western singer. "I love him and whatever happens I'll stick by him,""she sobbed as the sound of Tammy Wynette's *Stand by Your Man* appeared to echo through the air. Her man was Willie Johnston, the player at the centre of the first significant drugs scandal in the history of Scottish football, and a figure of such sentimental intensity, he should have played for Nashville.

The passage of time has played outrageous tricks on Willie Johnston. Long after his retirement from football, he is barely remembered for his flamboyant career and unique repertoire of skills. Instead, Willie Johnston will always be the player sent home in disgrace from Scotland's disastrous World Cup campaign in Argentina, found guilty of taking banned drugs in Scotland's ill-fated opening game against Peru.

The details of Johnston's drug incident have been lost in the mists of history. For most of us all that remains is a fleeting memory of news bulletins of the dejected player arriving at Heathrow Airport to face a miserable future as one half of a very well-worn football joke. Scotland had a great new strike force: Jinky on one wing and Junkie on the other.

Nearly 25 years and thousands of miles separated Willie Johnston's expulsion from the World Cup and the night of 23 December 2000 when two St Johnstone strikers, George O'Boyle and Kevin Thomas, were accused of recreational drug abuse and became the first players to be sacked by their clubs. As newspapers tied themselves in knots moralising about the sinning Saints, they invariably cast back to Willie Johnston and the blight of drugs in top class sport.

There was of course a fundamental difference, although when the word 'drug' is in play, subtle distinction tends to get bludgeoned beneath the weight of moral rhetoric. Johnston was accused of taking performance-enhancing drugs while the St Johnstone renegades were accused of snorting cocaine at a Christmas party. So history will record that Johnston was doing it for his country, while O'Boyle and Thomas were supposedly doing 'disco dandruff' in the bogs of

His image directly appealed to the hard core of Scotland's Tartan Army, a group of supporters whose tabloid image at the time was more notorious than the Visigoths

That Bar, a Perth nightspot. For one, drugs was all about the game; for the others the game was all about drugs. Take your pick.

Although the Willie Johnston drug scandal in Argentina plays such an integral part in the tragi-comedy of Scottish football, very few people can recount the circumstances that led to the player being banned for life. He took drugs – we know that – but what drugs? Crack, heroin, cocaine, speed, or dope?

No, that would have been too unambiguous a crime to cast before a Scottish court. Johnston's offence surrounded a drug called Reactivin, which in the days after the controversy broke was described variously as a pep pill, a pick-me-up, an anti-depressant, a psycho-motor stimulant and bizarrely "a substance normally taken for post-natal depression". When he admitted his offence to the SFA, poor Willie told them he had taken the drug to alleviate hay fever. If only he had the foresight to say he'd felt down since he gave birth, things might have been different. Not even the SFA would have been cruel enough to throw the book at a depressed dad.

The shortest fuse

Willie Johnston was a typical product of Scotland's working-class football heritage. Raised in Fife near Jim Baxter's birthplace, he worked as a pit-boy in the collieries, and established his early reputation with one of the great mining teams of the Fife Junior League, Lochore Welfare. As a teenager he signed for Rangers, winning a League Cup Winner's medal at 17, and establishing himself as a prominent newcomer in the Scotland youth team.

In a long and controversial career in football, which included spells with West Bromwich Albion, Vancouver Whitecaps and Birmingham City, Johnston finally retired in his 39th year still nimble enough to be a regular in Hearts first team. But it was his two spells at Rangers, where he was affectionately nicknamed 'Bud' that the mercurial Johnston established a reputation as a daring winger with a short emotional fuse. Sent off 20 times in his career, Johnston is a surprisingly quiet and tender man who lashed out at opponents, either on the spur of the moment or in the heartfelt belief that rational behaviour was for lesser talents.

Johnston was an explosive winger, an athlete with such a burst of natural speed that he once competed in the professional athletes' New Year dash, the Powderhall Sprint. Beyond that he was a showman, a player in the tradition of Alex James, Charlie Tully and Peter 'Ma Ba' McKenna, players who believed their calling was not simply to beat defenders but to

O'Boyle feels a proper Charlie after the drugs allegation

Johnston's sporadic acts of violence became so common they were almost obligatory

humiliate them in public.

Along with his contemporaries Willie Henderson and Jimmy Johnstone, Willie Johnston formed a formidable troika of wee wingers whose precocious 'tanner-ba' skills provoked comparison with the diminutive wizards of Scotland's most famous past. 'Bud' was the end of the assembly line, one of the last wee wingers the game produced before tactical reorganisation and a change in athletic stature turned his breed into a piece of football nostalgia. The breed still exists today, but they have been accommodated into the tactical matrix of midfield duty, and would blush if anyone called them wingers.

Wingers have a wicked vulnerability that makes them emotionally prone to scandal and the myths that grew up around Willie Johnston are incredible. His blistering turn of speed, cavalier attitude and rank bad discipline made him an instant hit with the fans and yet another scourge for the authorities to cope with. In his first few years at Rangers, he was sent off for striking five different opponents. In a tense cup tie a rival fan threw a can at him and in a moment of pantomime Bud picked up the can, motioned a greeting of 'cheers' to the terracing and drank some of the can's unknown contents.

Body trapped in two minds

Like so many of his kind, Bud had a split personality. Off the field he was a quiet family man, but with the ball at his feet and open space in front of him he became a demon. In the land where the SFA was sheriff, Johnston was Billy the Kid, a bandit in pursuit of an early bath. His image directly appealed to the hard core of Scotland's Tartan Army, a group of supporters whose tabloid image at the time was more notorious than the Visigoths.

In his second spell at Rangers, Johnston's sporadic acts of violence became so common they were almost obligatory. In a game against Aberdeen, he was sent off for the 13th time in his career for fouling John McMaster, and the Pittodrie player was taken to hospital with neck injuries. Two months later in a game against Hearts he moved down the human anatomy, this time fouling the opposition full-back Steve Hamilton, who was helped off the pitch with stud marks on his stomach.

The grazed posterior

Ironically, Johnston's lawless image endeared as much as it repelled. He was obviously a player who was easily unhinged, but in the odd chemistry of Scotland's football psyche his recklessness made him a dangerous if likeable rogue.

When Bud moved to West Bromwich Albion in 1976, he found himself in deep trouble after a game against Brighton, when he was sent off for kicking a referee. When latter-day misfits like Paolo Di Canio, the Celtic winger who moved south to Sheffield and then West Ham, outraged English football when he pushed a referee, it was clear the English had eradicated Bud Johnston from their collective memory.

Fortunately for Johnston, his kick only grazed the posterior of a leading

In a tense cup tie a rival fan threw a can at him and in a moment of pure pantomime, Bud picked up the can, motioned a greeting of 'cheers' to the terracing and drank some of the can's unknown contents

League official, Derek Lloyd of Worcester, and he was banned for only five matches. In what must be the most liberal judgement ever handed down by a football authority, the FA disciplinary committee decided it was unintentional. "If Johnston had deliberately intended an attack on the referee," the committee reported, "his right foot would not have missed the target."

Along with the bearded maestro Archie Gemmill, Johnston was the undisputed star of Scotland's 1978 World Cup squad. In the team's acclimatisation tour of Latin America, he kicked his way into the public's imagination and sowed the seeds of notoriety, which eventually led to his life ban.

The tour was tarred with controversy from the outset. Scotland's first game against Chile in Santiago coincided with international opposition to the Pinochet dictatorship and its appalling human rights violations. The stadium chosen for the game was literally the killing fields – a place where supporters of the deposed left-wing Allende government had been tortured and assassinated. Although Scotland's trades union movement opposed the game, it went ahead and the players stripped in changing rooms with bullet holes along the wall.

Scotland stuffed Chile and salvaged a victory out of the mouth of repression; a triumph for the left-wing, with Willie Johnston on show.

But it was in the following game against Argentina in Buenos Aires that Johnston really stole the show. In a display of breathtaking arrogance he virtually destroyed the career of the Argentinean defender Vincente Pernia, whom he tormented with twisting runs and terrific ball skills. In a moment of desperation, the defeated Pernia struck out at Johnston, the inevitable fight ensued and the two were sent off.

The humiliated Pernia never played for Argentina again and the normally partisan crowd jeered the referee for dismissing Johnston. In a stroke he had become the most famous footballer in the much-fancied Scotland side.

The roots of the Willie Johnston drug scandal had been firmly planted.

Just say no

If the St Johnstone drugs scandal a quarter of a century on had any roots, it was those of the peroxide blondes who lean precariously along the bar at Perth's designer pub That Bar.

Reach out and touch Bud Johnston's hand

It was nearly Christmas. Office parties were in full swing. St Johnstone's injured players were enjoying their Xmas bash. Anyone with crutches, limps and season tickets to Lilleshall sports injury clinic was warmly welcome. The club's physiotherapist Nick Summersgill had assembled his crocks for Christmas good cheer, and talk of torn tendons was gripping the crowded bar. The Perth club was scheduled to play an SPL game against Motherwell at McDiarmid Park the next day and the players who had escaped injury were tucked up in bed for the night.

According to reports, two of the injured players, the former Linfield,

O'Boyle had been dubbed a 'love-rat' for leaving his wife and moving in with a glamorous shop assistant

Bordeaux and Dunfermline striker George O'Boyle and his team mate Kevin Thomas were allegedly crushed into a cubicle snorting a white powder when the physio came a-calling. Before you could snap a cruciate ligament, the players supposedly told him to "fuck off" and the scene was set for a protracted and infamous scandal.

The Perth club sacked the players, an SPL appeal sided with the banished duo, and Saints chairman Geoff Brown was left facing the embarrassing consequences of opening his arms to welcome back two prodigal sons who only a month before he had unceremoniously booted out of the club.

One snapshot showed Thomas participating in a 'say no to drugs' charity event … now it had scandalous cachet

That Bar in Perth, allegedly host to that incident in those toilets

Although it should not be used in evidence against them, O'Boyle and Thomas had already attracted the promiscuous glances of the Scottish tabloid press. O'Boyle had been dubbed a 'love-rat' for leaving his wife and moving in with a glamorous shop assistant who worked in Benettons in Perth. The ever-vigilant press claimed that the shaven-headed O'Boyle had charmed her as he shopped for children's clothes.

Thomas's brush with scandal was grubbier. As a rising star in a famous BP Youth Cup-winning Hearts team the striker played alongside the cream of the Tynecastle crop, including Gary Locke and Paul Ritchie. But his moment of fame came in the most pernicious of circumstances, when it was revealed that he was sharing a sexual partner with the Hibernian full-back Willie Miller. It was a twos-up that divided Auld Reekie and the players clashed at a tetchy Edinburgh derby, exchanging blows up the tun-

nel. What else they exchanged up the tunnel should be left to the reader's imagination, and the laboratories of Napier University.

St Johnstone called and then cancelled a press conference, alerting journalists that a big story was breaking. It leaked that two players, later identified as O'Boyle and Thomas, had been accused of taking a recreational class 'A' drug in a bar in Perth. The players denied the accusations and a lengthy and acrimonious dispute took place over the subsequent months.

The St Johnstone drug debacle divided football. Some thought the club had acted promptly to protect the image of their youth academy. Others felt they had overreacted. The press had a field day, digging up previously innocent photos, which now seemed incriminating. One snapshot showed Thomas participating in a 'say no to drugs' charity event. In truth it was one of those photo-sessions that footballers are hustled into on a daily basis but now it had scandalous cachet.

As the Perth drug scandal unfolded it became increasingly clear that St Johnstone had taken the zero-tolerance approach, showing none of the touchy-feely sympathy that the other Saints, St Mirren, had shown when their fallen idol, Barry Lavety was embroiled in a previous drug scandal, involving the club drug ecstasy.

The portly St Mirren striker Lavety had set a redemptive tone for the abuse of recreational drugs in Scottish football. Lavety had been caught out at

a rave in an Ayrshire nightclub and was seen taking ecstasy. He was not alone. At the time the designer club drug was epidemic in Scotland and several unexplained deaths had made it a controversial substance guaranteed to ignite a flame of condemnation in the tabloid press.

Confess and be saved

There is little room for alternative opinion on drugs in Scottish football; the cant and double-speak that surrounds the subject would shame even the most flagrant hypocrite. There is only one response: drugs are bad, so bad you have to condemn them, flush them down the can, and vow never to watch *Superfly* again.

When St Mirren realised they were on a hiding to nothing they arranged for Lavety to confess his sins, and in an act of astonishing over-reaction signed him into a drug rehab clinic in the Borders. Lavety appeared almost daily in the press, speaking as if he was a washed up Hollywood has-been or a drug ravished rock star. In fact he was a slightly overweight young Scot, good enough to play for St Mirren and periodically for Scotland Under-21s. Like many young people of the day had taken 'E' but unlike most he was a professional football player, and in the great tradition of Hampden Babylon generated more public interest that truthfully he should.

Lavety's misfortune was that the drug he took was relatively new and uniquely misunderstood by those who took it

Barry Lavety's bookcase

and those who didn't. Ecstasy-related deaths had gathered momentum in Scotland throughout the 1990s, giving the press a seemingly legitimate reason for hounding any public figure that strayed from the way of righteousness. The death of a young girl in Perth's Ice Factory nightclub provoked widespread outrage. If the drug had a hold in places like Perth, went the script, nowhere in Scotland was safe.

Ironically, the Ice Factory was owned by local entrepreneur John Bryden, who was also the licensee of That Bar, where George O'Boyle was to meet his fateful moment as Christmas came to Perth.

McCulloch's drunken night at the wheel came in a summer of mayhem which reassured doubters that Scotland's young players were not about to surrender the legacy of our scandalous past

Excited about his return, O'Boyle gave the press one of the classic quotes of modern Scottish football – "I haven't scored for 18 months"

The drinks are in us

A further twist was hidden in the tale of Hampden Babylon. At the height of the media's moralising about O'Boyle's reported drug abuse, the Rangers defender Fernado Ricksen was arrested for an alleged drink-driving offence. Commentators wondered which was worse: being wobbly on your feet at a nightclub or having impaired vision at the wheel of a car? But it was another footballer, found guilty of drink-driving that brought the irony of hypocrisy to St Johnstone's door. Marc McCulloch was a product of the very youth academy that the club was trying desperately to protect.

McCulloch was banned for three months for wrecking a string of vehicles as he drove home drunk, having lost control of his vehicle at 80 mph in a road near the half-built Scottish parliament. Although it is but a footnote in the moral narrative of drink and drugs, McCulloch was in fact the first ever player to be presented with an SPL trophy. As captain of St Johnstone's Under-21 title-winning team of 1999, he was presented with the trophy the week before Rangers scooped the main prize and was congratulated by SPL Chief Executive Roger Mitchell, who wished him well for the future.

McCulloch's drunken night at the wheel came in a summer of mayhem which reassured any doubters that Scotland's young players were not about to surrender the great legacy of our scandalous past. Kilmarnock's boy wonder Peter Canero – like McCulloch a Scotland Under-21 international – was rushed home from holiday after falling into a glass-case gaming machine in what was dismissed by manager Bobby Williamson, almost inevitably, as "horseplay". Meanwhile, another bad boy of Scottish football, Brian Carrigan, was briefly rescued from obscurity by Dundee United after being sacked by Stockport County after a drunken night out. According to reports, Carrigan had driven a cab away without the owner's permission. Intriguingly the court heard that the owner, an English taxi driver, was found injured in the passenger seat. No explanation was forthcoming and Carrigan was dispatched north to Tannadice where he was taken under the sobering wing of United's born-again bad boy Charlie Miller.

The panda was asking for it

As St Johnstone's most controversial season came to an end, McCulloch secured his future by apologising to the club and to the fans. His contriteness was in marked contrast to O'Boyle, who subsequently moved on to Bud Johnston's home town of Kirkcaldy where he was greeted by Raith Rovers fans as a bargain. Emerging from a long injury and

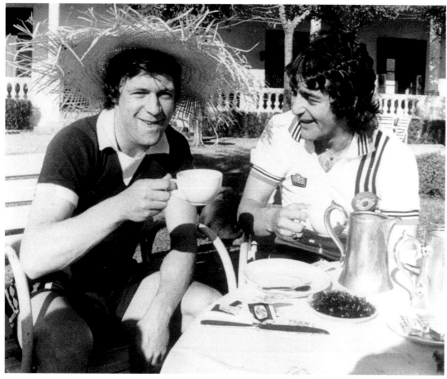

Home before the postcards: Johnston and Macari unaware of the impending crisis

excited about his return, O'Boyle told the press he couldn't wait to find the net, and gave them one of the classic quotes of modern Scottish football – "I haven't scored for 18 months."

As Raith Rovers began the 2001–02 season with O'Boyle up front, his former team mates travelled to Parkhead to watch treble-winning Celtic unfurl the SPL flag. The Perth team's captain Jim Weir, who had acted as one of the rock-solid professionals throughout the O'Boyle saga, was posted missing. He had been suspended from the match after being red carded the week before in a friendly at Love Street.

In an incident that not even a hallucinogenic hippy could have imagined, Weir had fought with the St Mirren mascot, Paisley Panda. The Panda was by then notorious in Scottish football, having once taunted Morton fans with a giant deodorant spray and on this occasion had carried a 'Spot The Arab' sign, which he pointed at the St Johnstone goalkeeper Alan Main. At the tail end of the previous season the former Dundee United keeper had conceded a soft goal that had relegated St Mirren, and the Buddies were not enamoured by his appearance at Love Street.

And so one of Scottish football's biggest drugs scandals ended in a surreal and chaotic way with O'Boyle back in football playing a few miles from Willie Johnston's pub. Meanwhile his former club captain was hallucinating on the very pitch that Barry Lavety had plied his trade by threatening to banjo a six-foot Panda. You can't get a weirder trip than that.

Ironically, the madness of the era had also gripped one of Scotland's greatest-ever young players, Derek Johnstone, a man who at 16 had scored for Rangers in the 1970 League Cup Final. By now a professional

The small yellow tablets coated in sugar and containing nothing more stimulating than a couple of stiff cups of coffee became the most bitter pill that Bud Johnston ever swallowed

commentator with Radio Clyde, Johnstone's tempestuous life led to a driving ban the same week that the O'Boyle drug case came to appeal. Johnstone was banned from driving after being breathalysed. To bring events full circle, he had been Bud's team mate at Ibrox, and had travelled with him on the ill-fated expedition to Argentina.

The eerie link
O'Boyle in the bogs, Lavety at a rave and Bud Johnston crying in Argentina.

Separated by decades but linked by the demon word drugs, and the unravelling narcotic confusions of scandal in small town Scotland.

The events that led to Johnston's life ban are steeped in confusion and appalling bad luck. The Scotland team had been instructed by the team's doctors to avoid taking any medicinal substances which might be banned by the laws of the game. But Johnston frequently took either smelling salts or the mild psycho-motor drug Reactivin at club level to make him more alert when he went out to play. Neither the salts nor the drug were illegal in either Scotland or England, and Johnston, along with other team mates, had taken them as part of their pre-match rituals on many occasions. In that

respect, Johnston's only crime was naivety.

As part of his emotive pre-match build up, Ally McLeod promised Scotland would dismantle Peru in their opening game in the 1978 finals. With England already out of the tournament, the British media were pursuing Scotland and hung on McLeod's every word. At an ill-advised and emotionally hyped press conference, McLeod announced to the world that Willie Johnston would "terrorise their full-backs", and the rest would be academic. It wasn't.

With Scotland, it never is.

Feeling unusually low and depressed from a bout of hayfever, Johnston did the natural thing and reached for a couple of Reactivins. The small yellow tablets coated in sugar and containing nothing more stimulating than a couple of stiff cups of coffee became the most bitter pill that Bud Johnston ever swallowed.

Johnston was dire. He played like he'd been on tranquillisers for a month and drifted out of the game into a deep and ineffectual sleep. His team mates were hardly conspicuous in their greatness; the team lost three goals and conceded the match to their massively underestimated opponents. Recriminations would come thick and fast, but not even the voracious

His wife picked up the phone believing it was an anniversary treat from her husband. Willie simply said, "I think I'll be home quicker than you imagine"

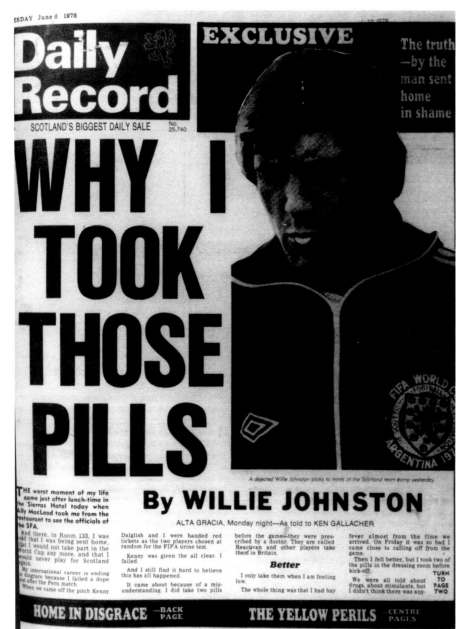

ESDAY June 6 1978

Daily Record

SCOTLAND'S BIGGEST DAILY SALE   No. 25,740

EXCLUSIVE

The truth —by the man sent home in shame

WHY I TOOK THOSE PILLS

A dejected Willie Johnston sticks to mints at the Scotland team camp yesterday.

By WILLIE JOHNSTON

ALTA GRACIA, Monday night—As told to KEN GALLACHER

THE worst moment of my life came just after lunch-time in the Sierras Hotel today when Ally MacLeod took me from the restaurant to see the officials of the SFA.

And there, in Room 133, I was told that I was being sent home, that I would not take part in the World Cup any more, and that I would never play for Scotland again.

My international career is ending in disgrace because I failed a dope test after the Peru match.

When we came off the pitch Kenny

Dalglish and I were handed red tickets as the two players chosen at random for the FIFA urine test.

Kenny was given the all clear. I failed.

And I still find it hard to believe this has all happened.

It came about because of a mis-understanding. I did take two pills

before the game—they were pres-cribed by a doctor. They are called Reactivan and other players take them in Britain.

Better

I only take them when I am feeling low.

The whole thing was that I had hay

fever almost from the time we arrived. On Friday it was so bad I came close to calling off from the game.

Then I felt better, but I took two of the pills in the dressing room before kick-off.

We were all told about drugs, about stimulants, but I didn't think there was any-

TURN TO PAGE TWO

HOME IN DISGRACE —BACK PAGE   **THE YELLOW PERILS** —CENTRE PAGES

Scottish press could have guessed what would happen next.

In keeping with standard FIFA prac-tice, officials walked on to the pitch and handed red coupons to two of the most famous Scottish players, Willie Johnston and Kenny Dalglish. Johnston was used to red cards, but this particular coupon was to signal a different kind of brush with authority, a sign that the player had been selected for a random dope test. The recurring problem of performance-enhancing drugs at the Olympic Games had set increasingly high standards at major tournaments. As Johnston passed his urine he reflected on the result. Sensing that his uncharacteristically quiet performance was a sign of dark-er times ahead, he wearily joked, "It would be typical if they found something."

They did. Bud Johnston was on drugs and the disastrous defeat by Peru was unfolding into one of Scottish football's biggest debacles.

But what had Bud actually taken? Not the hurried recreational drugs that began there life-cycle as a coca plant in the Peruvian mountains and ended up as crushed powder in a Perth toilet. It wasn't the cocaine that O'Boyle and Thomas allegedly were to take on the injured players' big night out in Perth. Nor was it the chemical underground that had lured St Mirren's Barry Lavety into the realm of ecstasy at a rave in Ayr.

It was the kind of drugs you could buy in a chemist's shop in Cupar. Ken the one I mean?

Late night high jinx

At 10pm on the night of the Peru game, Ally McLeod received a telegram at the Sierra Hotel at the team's training base in Alta Gracia. The telegram had come from FIFA's headquarters in Buenos Aires and informed the Scotland manger that one of his players, William Johnston, had traces of the proscribed drug Fencamsamin in his urine. At first Johnston denied it, in the sincere belief that he had not taken illegal substances, but when the doctor asked if he had taken Reactivin, Johnston endearingly replied in his strong Fife accent "Aye, but they're no drugs."

Confusion reigned in the Scotland camp. FIFA regulations permitted an appeal, a second urine test and an independent analysis. Many other countries would have grabbed at the straw, but with Johnston virtually admitting guilt, the SFA representatives were unwilling to appeal. The timing could not have been worse. Defeat by Peru was bad enough but the entire Scottish party had been invited to a reception with the Minister of Sport Denis Howell, a former referee and a declared opponent of drug abuse in sport.

In a night of increasingly frantic desperation the Scottish party was in meltdown. Rumours of the drug scandal were leaking by the hour. Out of the blue, the Scotland midfield schemer Don Masson, who had missed a penalty in the game against Peru, approached McLeod and admitted that he too had taken the banned drug. In a mood of increasing depression Johnston, a West Brom player at the time, rang home to Sutton Coldfield. Back home it was 6.30 am and ironically the morning of his wedding anniversary. His wife picked up the phone believing it was an anniversary treat from her husband. Willie simply said, "I think I'll be home quicker than you imagine."

Then the phone went dead.

Back in Argentina, Masson had been called in front of a hurriedly convened SFA meeting, where he confusingly changed his story. He claimed that he had only said he had taken the drugs as an act of loyalty to his friend and

The rules of rehab

Has there ever been a greater transformation in a footballer's image than that of Duncan Ferguson? The one time bad boy was hailed as a 'have-a-go hero' for banjoing an intruder at his home in Ormskirk. The former resident of Glasgow's Barlinnie prison was protecting his luxury villa and abiding by the moral code of suburbia – an Anglo's home is his castle.

A few years back, not even the most deranged bookie in Britain would have given odds on Duncan Ferguson becoming the good guy. It is the most outrageous turnaround since Jimmy Corkhill gave up heroin to become a teacher.

Curiously, Ferguson's transformation came at the same time as St Johnstone strikers George O'Boyle and Kevin Thomas faced the challenge of rebuilding their careers.

A motley crew of fans, football professionals and pundits reached for the moral machine gun and annihilated them, and months after the event perhaps it's time for reflection.

I confess from the outset that I do climb naturally to the pulpit. I can list a catalogue of 'mistakes' that I have made over the years and look forward to many more in the years to come. In fact, the last time I was drunk at a football match was in the company of the irrepressible George O'Boyle. We were in the clubhouse at Shamrock Rovers after a pre-season friendly in Dublin, and the bald maestro took a tenner off me in some duff game involving beer-mats.

> **The authorities have been caught flat-footed, forced to hide behind the weasel words of legal process – it would be unfair to comment until the matter is resolved, blah, blah, blah**

Like so many St Johnstone fans, I have totally confused views on the scandal. I wish it hadn't happened, but then again it's not often your team gets a bit of attention. The club has to protect its successful youth system, but the generation the club seeks to protect is more prone to drug abuse than O'Boyle's age group.

Yet again football has failed to grasp the extent of recreational drug abuse among players. The authorities have been caught flat-footed, forced to hide behind the weasel words of legal process – it would be unfair to comment until the matter is resolved, blah, blah, blah.

Some commentators have slagged off St Johnstone for being callous and uncaring. But in the cold realities of football, the money they save from sacking the two players allows them to pay wages to another signing target. Selfish fans will welcome this opportunity.

When Claudio Caniggia comes to play at Perth I happily hum along to the funky-junkie chants. I don't want George O'Boyle to be victimised but I am happy to victimise others.

The only logic I can fathom from the scandal is that fans are a shower of two-faced bandits who will twist any situation to suit their team. Anyone who says anything consistent about George O'Boyle's sacking is probably a drug counsellor first and a football fan second.

The key challenge for O'Boyle and Thomas is how they manage their rehabilitation. Kilmarnock's Andy McLaren transformed himself from a hopeless alcoholic to a born-again star, and in a less foolproof way Barry Ferguson has gone from street-lout to honourable club-captain. And if Duncan Ferguson can go from bad-boy to hero then there is hope for us all.

The one thing that I would always canvas against is the fake retribution that St Mirren's Barry Lavety was forced to undergo. Like thousands of his generation he took ecstasy at a rave. But he was hounded into a drug rehabilitation clinic even although it was obvious to all concerned that he was neither addicted nor a serious abuser of the drug. Lavety was a victim of an American habit – recanting through therapy or saying sorry at the clinic doors.

The only journey open to O'Boyle is the quiet, difficult and long road to transformation. Not for the media, not for the fans nor for the moral guardians that populate Scotland, but quite simply for himself.

room mate, Johnston. McLeod called the rest of the team together and asked the entire squad if they had access to prescribed drugs. Several other players owned up and the manager collected as many as two dozen pills from the squad.

The next day, racked by pressure, confusion and the desire to get something right, McLeod dumped the drugs in a field near the hotel. Scotland's trip to Argentina began with a wave of nationalist euphoria and ended in the complete ignominy of their exuberant manager scuttling around a field hiding pep pills.

almost every newspaper.

Bud Johnston the consummate and irrepressible winger had never been so alone.

Reduced to tears, exiled from his team mates and already banned from playing for his beloved Scotland for life, the victimised figure of Willie Johnston arrived back at Heathrow Airport to be met by his club manager Ron Atkinson. In an emotional reunion they hugged each other as West Brom's chairman Bert Millichip told the assembled press that Johnston's career at the Hawthorns was secure. Millichip told them that

"I feel like a leper, all they need to do now is put a bell round my neck"

The flower of Scotland had well and truly wilted.

"I feel like a leper"
The media thrived on Johnston's anxiety. On the morning of 5 June 1978 the press was alive with speculation. With England absent from the finals, the entire weight of the British media fell on Willie Johnston's head. He was smuggled out of the Scotland camp but it was only a matter of time when his pursuers caught up. At first Johnston was contrite and ashamed. "I am heart-broken," he said in one of the first press reports "I am a disgrace to myself and my country. I don't know how I am going to face my wife."

In what seemed like a bizarre dress rehearsal of the fate awaiting his near-namesake, the Olympic sprinter Ben Johnson, words like 'drugs', 'disgrace', 'cheat' and 'liar' recurred in

Johnston had not breached any of the club rules and was generally regarded as one of their most loyal players. In the whole sorry saga, West Bromwich Albion were one of the few parties to emerge with dignity.

Unlike the censorious and supremely moral SFA, they rallied round their player when he most needed their support.

Johnston was rushed away from the airport in a police motorcade. Over the next few days he was never out of the press and in one emotional moment he confided to a journalist that he felt betrayed by Scotland. "They are trying to sling mud at me to cover up the defeat by Peru," he said, rising to his own defence and pointing a brave if belated finger back at the SFA. "I feel like a leper, all they need to do now is put a bell round my neck." If they kept bells at Park Gardens they might have.

Over the years football authorities have become obsessed with rooting out drug abuse in the game. After the Johnston saga, FIFA demanded a far-reaching investigation into the misuse of drugs in English League football. For weeks it threatened to be a cess pit of scandal, and not to be outdone the controversial English striker Stan Bowles, whose behaviour over the years made him seem like a surrogate Scot, admitted that he frequently took drugs.

Flying round the world

Bowles was awarded a big cheque from a tabloid newspaper and if his own self-professed myths are a guide-line it could have been squandered at the nearest bookies. The more reliable FIFA enquiry found no significant evidence of the misuse of drugs. Unlike the athletics scene where the use of anabolic steroids was rife, football had very few cages to rattle; almost all the significant incidences of drug abuse were overseas.

In 1969 a doping scandal at FC Bologna in Italy led to the entire team being found guilty. In Uruguay the following year two internationalists admitted using an exotic African drug and in the World Cup prior to Argentina, FIFA banned the Haitian internationalist Ernst Joseph for taking the proscribed drug phenlmetrazin.

Since then the serious pushing has taken place in Colombia where the cocaine cartels have literally ruined football by using Medellin and FC Cali as laundering centres for drug money. Sadly the Colombian defender, Andreas Escobar, was killed after he had conceded an own goal in the World Cup Finals in the USA. To this day the rumour persists that the Colombian drug cartels had bet heavily on the outcome of the match.

By 2000 drugs were part of the everyday discourse of professional football. The England captain Tony Adams stole a march on the market when he confessed to serial substance abuse in his biography *Addicted* and then opened a rehab-clinic for recovering footballers.

Set next to the assassination of players, managers and referees in Colombia, Willie Johnston was a choirboy. The traumas of Argentina would have dampened a lesser spirit than Bud's. But the wee winger from Fife bounced back in a way that says much for the survivalist instincts in the human spirit. After a successful career in England, Willie Johnston followed the exodus of ageing British professional players to the US Soccer League, where he joined the Canadian team Vancouver Whitecaps.

Back to his best

Johnston was the shining star in an excellent Whitecaps side which included former English internationalists Alan Ball and Jon Sammels, his performances put an estimated 6,000 on the team's home gate; within a season Johnston had led them to the Soccer Bowl final against Tampa Bay Rowdies. But it was in a game against the famous New York Cosmos that Willie Johnston rediscovered himself.

Never fully attuned to the intricate histories of football, the New York team sided a former Argentinean international, and instructed him to mark the mercurial Johnston out of the game. In a display of spiteful professionalism, the Argentinean defender pursued Johnston like a villainous Latin American stereotype from *Roy Of The Rovers* trying to unsettle the emotional Scot with the scurrilous taunt "Droogs, droogs, Johnston swallow droogs."

Sick of being subjected to the Argentinean's taunts Johnston simply replied, "Come near me sunshine and you'll be swallowing your teeth." Later in the game he was sent off for his part in a vicious brawl. The leper had long gone and the real Bud Johnston was back. ◊

Sick of being subjected to the Argentinean's taunts Johnston simply replied,

"Come near me sunshine and you'll be swallowing your teeth"

12

PUFF DADDY PLAYS FOR PARTICK

Russell Latapy looked in the mirror and liked what he saw. His denim jacket was fashionably baggy, like the ragamuffin reggae singers he listened to as a teenager. His T-shirt was crisp white, his hair cropped short.

He had been in Scotland for a couple of years and it was time to think about the future. Hibs had had their best season for 30 years and were in the Cup final. A new contract was being dangled in front of him. He could either stay at a club where he was already a legend or try to hustle a contract down south where his childhood friend Dwight Yorke was a star at Manchester United. He liked his penthouse apartment in Stockbridge but he was one of football's much travelled band of modern professionals and he knew that to make decent dough you simply had to move on.

But as Latapy gazed in the mirror a much bigger decision confronted him:

baseball caps. He knew he would wear the pale blue one. But how should it be worn? Increasingly he favoured pulling the cap moodily down over his eyes. That's the way most of his team-mates were wearing them now. Even wee John O'Neil had a baseball hat, even big Mixu wore one the right way round. But Russell still hankered after the past.

The bad boy look of ragamuffin rap had Russell Latapy in its grip. He turned the baseball cap 180 degrees until the peak followed the line of his neck. It was maybe a fading fashion but like a Frank Sauzee free-kick, a fight with Alex McLeish or a goal away at Tynecastle, some things just felt right.

Latapy picked up his mobile phone and mimed, using it as an imaginary microphone. He watched his reflection and pretended he was an old-skool rapper, boasting about sex, guns and sucker MCs. Within an hour he would be at Rick's Bar and Ali G could kiss his butt.

When a Lothian and Borders patrol car chased a Volkswagen Beetle through the late night streets of Edinburgh they had no inclination who was inside. From a distance it appeared that the driver of the reckless car was a black man wearing a baseball hat. But there were passengers too, and something resembling tentative lust appeared to be taking place in the back seat. Inside the car was Russell Latapy, Dwight Yorke and two local girls they had met on the dancefloor at Eye Candy, the VIP area of Edinburgh's Mercado nightclub.

Hibernian Football Club was about to face one of its most dispiriting few days. Not since the publication of Irvine Welsh's *Trainspotting* and the adventures of Begbie, Rent Boy and Spud had the Easter Road club been tangled in such a web of scandal and disarray. Not since the chaotic years when the Hibs casual terrorised Scottish football had the club's name

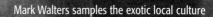
Mark Walters samples the exotic local culture

The hip-hop Hibees

been linked with trendy clothes.

In the back of Russell Latapy's car, his childhood friend Yorke was embracing a Royal Bank of Scotland employee, and it wasn't a fixed interest mortgage he had in mind. Yorke's girl-friend, the glamour-model Jordan with her infamous 32FF bust, was elsewhere, and the Manchester United striker's eyes had wandered towards talent of a local kind.

Two clubbers at Eye Candy had taken photographs with a party cam-era, a dispute over the snaps had ensued, and Latapy, defending his pal's honour, and trying to prevent the photos ending up in the newspa-

Not since the chaotic years when the Hibs casual terrorised Scottish football had the club's name been linked with trendy clothes

pers, decided to chase the clubbers through Edinburgh in his car.

The fatal flaw

There was one small flaw in the plan – the elixir of Hampden Babylon. Latapy had become acclimatised to life in Scotland and – not to shirk the

issue – he was pissed. When the local patrol car stopped him in his tracks he was three times over the legal limit, and one thing was now guaranteed. The photos would appear in the news-paper for weeks to come. What's more they would be sent round the world, even to Trinidad and Tobago where

Latapy and Yorke were household names.

In Britain, Dwight Yorke was a superstar whose relationship with Jordan allowed him to rub shoulders with the charisma couple Manchester United team-mate David Beckham and his wife Posh Spice, and the Liverpool player Jamie Redknapp and his wife Louise of the pop group Eternal.

Latapy was famous in Scotland and frequently rubbed shoulders with the soccer glitterati – like Steven Tweed and his wife.

Back home in Trinidad Latapy was a living legend, the most capped player in the country's history; in fact the most capped footballer in the world. He had played for Trinidad well over 125 times, although some Caribbean inter-island matches earned him a cap, even though they were no more important than the Inter-Toto.

Break all the rules

As a playmaker Latapy had ignited a rejuvenated Hibs side, helping them climb out of the First Division to become genuine title contenders for most of the 2000–1 season. Along with the former Marseilles schemer Frank Sauzee, Latapy's name was virtually etched in the collective memory of Hibs fans, up there with the Famous Five, Alex Cropley and the Stanton era.

Somehow and for no good reason, other than the mercenary shifts of modern football, Latapy blew it. He announced he was leaving the club in the crucial run-in for a European place with Hibs facing a cup final with Celtic. Out of favour with his manager and with half a mind on his next club, his form dipped. Then Dwight Yorke rang him looking for a night out, away from the paparazzi, somewhere quite like Edinburgh.

Latapy was arrested, charged with drunk driving and unceremoniously

dumped by Hibs. Manager Alex McLeish had bent over backwards to give his fading star the benefit of every reasonable doubt. But this time there was no way back. Latapy had played his last game at Easter Road and it was made obvious that he would not be welcome at the Cup final.

Frank Sauzee captured the spirit of the controversy when he rushed to defend his team-mate. He told the *Daily Record*, "Right now its very hard for the wee man. But that's life and we learn every day."

Sauzee spoke like a true philosopher, like a true Frenchman. He even had

the dignity to fashion his philosophy so that it would easily digestible for Hibs fans. Even Jean Paul Sartre would have struggled with the concept of *the wee man*. One thing is certain, Latapy will never be remembered by his French colleague as the *oui man*.

Hibs manager Alex McLeish, who had spent the previous few months defending Latapy in the face of press accusations that he was no longer trying, ran out of patience and announced that Latapy had played his last game in a Hibs jersey. McLeish denied the drunk driving offence was

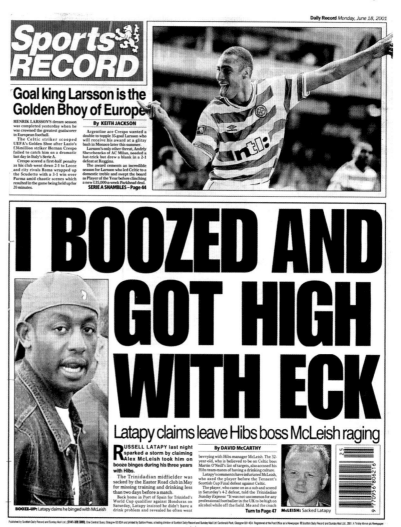

Despite evidence to the contrary, Latapy claimed that he and McLeish were drinking buddies

Jaffa – will he crumble in the box?

He wore the trademark baseball hat – and strolled into training like Puff Daddy in Partick

to blame. Fending off any legal claims against the club, he claimed it was purely a football matter.

"I think he knows he blew his chance," McLeish told reporters. "He won't play in the final of the cup. He has broken the rules. We don't allow players to drink 48 hours before a game and he broke the rules."

Such was the strained relationship between player and manger that the supportive McLeish put the boot into his sacked star. Anticipating the final a few days later against Celtic he said with withering contempt.

"We have played Celtic without him before," McLeish moaned, "when he was on holiday – sorry that was a slip

– when he was on international duty."

Feed the world, Let them know it's kick off time

The Scottish game had changed out of all recognition during the period Russell Latapy played at Hibs. Not only had the league transformed into the corporate SPL, pay television had arrived and the Bosman ruling meant that players now had contractual rights broadly in line with most other employees. Put simply they could move on more or less when it suited them.

The free movement of football talent brought about another significant change. Suddenly, and often with implausible outcomes, footballers

from around the world descended on Scotland. In the week of Latapy's arrest, Didier Agathe from the Reunion Islands was a right-wing sensation with champions Celtic. Only two players outshone him: Henrik Larrsson, a mixed race Swede whose father was from Cape Verde, and Lubo Moravcik, a gifted playmaker from the Czech Republic. Rangers had over ten Dutchmen on their books. And the further you looked the more romantic it all seemed.

Before he moved to Celtic, St Johnstone's languorous talisman was Mohammed 'Momo' Sylla, a French-African. Aberdeen fans wore red fezs in appreciation of their Moroccan stars Richard Belebed and Hiacham 'Zero' Zerouali. Unbelievably, Dundee had plunged into the transfer market and built a team around Argentinean stars like Fabian Caballero and Claudio Caniggia. And for most of the late '90s, former Angolan 'war-baby' Jose Quitongo dived at the feet of defenders across Scotland playing variously for Hamilton, St Mirren and Hearts.

After successive disappointments, which took them down the divisions, Partick Thistle, who had once traded on the image of being the Maryhill Magyars, looked to Africa and signed the Namibian internationalist Quentin Jacobs. He even wore the trademark baseball hat – and strolled into training like Puff Daddy in Partick.

But the arrival of black players in Scottish football was by no means a recent phenomenon. There is a hidden history, a story that makes Alex Haley's slave classic *Roots* read like a Mills and Boon paperback.

Yes we have no bananas !

One of the great delusions of Scottish society is the widespread belief that Scotland is a tolerant and welcoming country and that racism is a problem confined to England's green unpleasant land. Mark Walters's arrival at Ibrox just after Christmas 1987 blew the whistle on that myth. Week after week, the young black winger was subjected to a barrage of racial abuse, as prejudice squads at Parkhead, Tynecastle and Fir Park threw bananas, chanted like monkeys and banged the jungle drums in a desperate bid to put the player off his stride.

Mark Walters could not have chosen

a banana off the pitch. The Celtic fanzine *Not The View* was sufficiently appalled to write an angry editorial dismissing the incidents as the work of fascists and bigots who had no place at Parkhead. The Man From Delmonte refused to comment.

Flight of the Black Arrow
The Celtic fans who berated Walters had a conveniently short memory. Less

Walters – demonstating that his left leg really was just for standing on

Within days of Walters' arrival he was nicknamed Jaffa: black on the outside, orange on the inside

a more challenging game to begin his career in Scotland. He played his first game against Celtic in a New Year derby match at Parkhead, rekindling a long time rivalry with Celtic's Paul McStay, which had stretched back to their schooldays. Walters had been the star of a highly fancied England team that had lost to the Scottish Schools' team captained by McStay in the annual schoolboy international. But this time it was for real.

Walters was black in blue – a gifted young forward from Aston Villa who had yet to learn that Old Firm rivalry is the stuff of strange fruit. Within days of his arrival he was nicknamed Jaffa: black on the outside, orange on the inside. According to flamboyant press reports in the days around Walter's debut, soft fruit was sold out in Glasgow's East End as the less pious members of Celtic's hardcore support stocked up with ammunition. At various moments throughout the game, bananas were thrown at the Rangers winger and in one tense moment Walters bent down to tentatively move

than 30 years before, the club had enlightened post-war Scottish football by signing a black American striker from the US amateur team Chicago Maroons. His name was Giles Heron. Within days of his debut he became known as The Black Arrow and by an odd twist of history he was to enter Parkhead legend when his son, the radical singer Gil Scott-Heron, had international hit records with protest pop songs like *The Bottle* and *Johannesburg*.

Heron only stayed at Parkhead for a couple of seasons, long enough to become embittered by unfriendly Scottish winters and enchanted by the attention of a local Glasgow girl called Margaret whom he met at the dancing. The couple are happily married and live in Detroit, where Giles Heron still enjoys ridiculing his black friends with the word 'darkie' which he relishes saying in a pantomime Scots accent.

Heron's son has established himself as one of the major musical commentators in modern black America. His songs frequently convey anti-racist

The Black Arrow in the green hoops

since the 1950s, he too had to endure systematic racism from opposition players and fans. Soon after his arrival in Glasgow he admitted that he'd never experienced race-hate like it and told the press: "The racial abuse I've suffered in Scotland is far worse that anything I had to put up with in England or Italy."

There has long been a paranoid suspicion at Parkhead that most first class referees are masons, but Elliot's first season raised another worrying spectre. In his previous spell with Pisa he had only been cautioned once for a foul on Napoli's Diego Maradona. In his first season with Celtic he was booked 16 times. Was it the insidious work of the Ku Klux Klan?

The history of black footballers in Scotland is a long if interrupted one. The legacy stretches as far back as 1898, when John 'Darky' Walker of Leith Town signed for Hearts. Walker, a product of Leith's trading links with Africa, played a blinder in his debut against Hibs. In the following week he became the first black player to score in the Scottish League in a 3–1 win over St Bernards.

Vodka Vic Meets Super-Fly

Race relations in Scottish football have

sentiments and dramatise moments in the history of civil rights. If he was asked his opinion of Walters it would probably provoke comparisons with trailblazing events in the history of the civil rights movement. Walters was Ibrox's equivalent of Rosa Parks, the black woman who refused to take her segregated seat on a Deep South bus. He was the Ibrox answer to Willie Meredith, the first black student to be registered at the all-white University of Mississippi. Or if comparisons become badly derailed then Walters was the Martin Luther King of the Copeland Road End.

Walters was soon joined in the demonology of Old Firm football by another English-born black, the former Aston Villa and Pisa defender Paul Elliot. When Elliot arrived at Parkhead and became the first Celtic soul bhoy

'Darky' Walker's first goal ... in 1898

"He is now our player unless he disappears between Shrewsbury and here, so we have sent a driver with him to make sure he comes back"

inevitably thrown up their own welter of scandals. None more so than the life and times of Victor Kasule, Scotland's most notorious black player. Although the bold Victor never made it to the high altar of football, and has spent most of his career turning tricks at Albion Rovers, Meadowbank Thistle, Hamilton Accies and beyond, he has built up a fearsome reputation. Walters quickly assimilated into the Scottish game by dressing in a kilt and enraging Celtic fans by kissing the Rangers' strip when he scored. He was even sent off in an Old Firm derby on Mad Sunday: 17 March 1991. But his achievements paled alongside Vic Kasule. Vic threw his life and soul into the scandalous side of Scottish football. In the words of rap crews from the ganglands of East LA, Vic was NWA: a nigger with attitude. One by one he wound up managers and bit by bit his misbehaviour made him a player to avoid. In a hectic spell of little more than a few months, the Glasgow-born striker managed the unbelievable feat of being disciplined by three separate clubs. After a period playing in the Scottish First Division, he was transferred south to Shrewsbury Town. But his period at that bastion of sexual liberalism, Gay Meadow, was riddled with difficulties. Frustrated with Vic's antics, the Shrewsbury manager Ian McNeil sent him on a month's loan to Darlington, hoping to recoup most of the £35,000 he had paid Meadowbank

for the wayward Scot. It was not to be. Before the month was up Vic had been sent packing. Darlington's manager Brian Little found him an even bigger handful. "There's nothing wrong with Victor the footballer," he told a local newspaper, "but his activities off the field have proved a disruptive factor." Inevitably Kasule's exploits at Shrewsbury involved other Scottish players. Such was their notoriety amongst fans that the club's Scottish posse – which also included Alan Irvine and Dougie Bell – frequently

made damning headlines in the local press. One issue of the *Shrewsbury Chronicle* contained a piece of poetic doggerel which ended with an unforgettable rhyming couplet, "Irvine, Kasule and Bell. They make the manager's life pure hell." The comment provoked Alan Irvine to try to rescue his image. "The rest of the stuff didnae bother me," said Irvine, distancing himself with every word, "it was being associated with Victor." In a cynical homage to Caledonia, the Shrewsbury fans named their fanzine *A Double Scotch*, a lasting reminder that their greatest era had little to do with football.

Lambie to the slaughter

Who was tough enough to tame Vic? The next manager to step in was John Lambie, then manager of Hamilton Accies, but the transfer was destined to be a nightmare, with the Accies secretary claiming to have "signed whole teams quicker than I have signed Vic

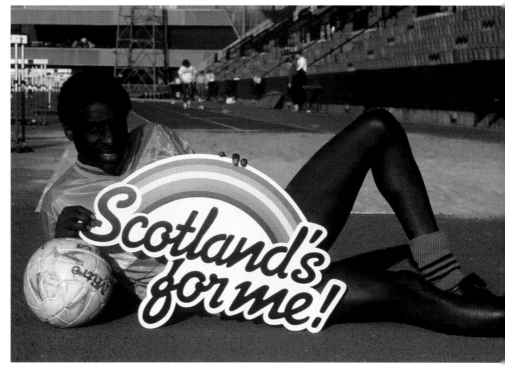

… because I can't get a game in England

Celtic soul bhoy sells double glazing

The black footballers who have graced Scotland have understood the true principles of assimilation

Kasule." On the day of his £15,000 move, Kasule drove back to Scotland but forgot his signing-on forms. The SFA refused to accept the photocopies and Vic had to return south. In a moment of sheer frustration, a Hamilton spokesman said: "He is now our player unless he disappears between Shrewsbury and here, so we have sent a driver with him to make sure he comes back."

In the grand tradition of blaxploitation cinema, Kasule was the John Shaft of the substitutes' bench, blazing his way through the ghettos of the First Division, with the old super-fly motto 'I'm Gonna Get You Sucka'.

He paid one final visit to Shrewsbury. Without informing his new club Vic headed south again, this time he became involved in a street brawl in Shrewsbury's Copthorne Road, where he allegedly became entangled with a local youth and, Vic being Vic, the police arrived, accusations were made and by the end of the night there was a warrant out for Kasule's arrest. Lambie was beside himself. He immediately imposed a record club fine of £4,000 on the forward by withholding a substantial part of his signing-on fee.

Baptised with the nickname 'Vodka Vic' by doting Hamilton fans, Kasule's period with the team was sadly short lived. In what *The Guardian* has described as "an epic itinerary" of a career, Kasule left Hamilton for Finland and then Malta. During season 1989–90 he set a dubious record of playing in the English, Scottish and Irish League in the same season and

will always be remembered at Shrewsbury as the player who over-turned a team mate's car on the way to buy a paper.

The Elliot saga

Kasule's dispute with Hamilton was by no means the only scandal involving Scotland's small posse of black players. Jim McLean, the manager of Dundee United, faced one of his most perplexing managerial decisions when a local clothes store rang the club to complain that their striker Raphael Meade had done a runner and left an unpaid bill of £870. In the months before he left United to play in Denmark, Meade had run up a bill at McGill Brothers, a Dundee department store. The club paid.

Meade's tracks were barely covered when Paul Elliot sprang into action. In an unprecedented move, he took out a lawsuit against his own club. Towards the end of July 1990 at Glasgow Sheriff Court he sued Celtic for over £157,000 in what was delicately described as a "matter that could not be settled amicably". The Celtic director and club solicitor Jim Farrell refused to expand on Elliot's claim, arguing it was *sub judice*.

The dispute between Celtic and Paul Elliot came at a difficult time for the club. Facing yet another crisis in the boardroom, and enduring an unbelievable slump in form, Celtic first-footed 1991 well adrift of Rangers in the league. The Elliot case was cold comfort; he was one of the very few success stories at the club and his periodic raids on opposition goalmouths were one of the few silver linings in Celtic's threadbare season.

The Paul Elliot dispute reputedly centred on a house that had been part of his package of transfer demands. The very mention of mysterious houses undoubtedly sent a ghostly shiver down the spine of several

Scottish football clubs. In January of that year Chelsea were fined and censured by the English FA when a house in Bridge of Allan near Stirling became the subject of a dispute between the club and the ex-Rangers player Graham Roberts. Accused of making illegal payments to its players, Chelsea were forced to lick their wounds in the knowledge that the Roberts's house was acid indigestion.

Elliot's success at Celtic was shaded by the peculiar circumstances of his dispute with the club. Even in the weird world of Hampden Babylon it is unusual for a player to sue his club and then in the next breath vow undying loyalty to their crumbling cause on the field. But Elliot showed remarkable commitment to Celtic on the pitch, and when the dispute erupted he confounded normal football logic by performing more wholeheartedly than at any previous stage in his career. When Elliot reflects back on his days at Celtic, the case of the haunted house will probably fade away.

Whatever its problems, Scottish football has shown an ingenious ability to offer the hand of friendship to outsiders. In Hampden Babylon all races are created equal; when they pull on a football shirt, ethnicity and colour evaporate into insignificance, and they become part of the glorious brotherhood of scandal.

The black footballers who have graced Scotland have had a decency and a dignity that should not go unheralded; they have understood the true principles of assimilation They have not been shy to swerve past bouncers on their way to their goal. So let a Baptist choir fill the heavens with the sound of an uplifting Negro spiritual because there on the floor grinding is a boy with a baseball hat on backwards. And standing at the bar is Vodka Vic.

Free at last, free at last, good God almighty free at last. ◊

Scarred culture

Two teams approached the last World Cup finals with fears about their strike force. One ended up taking a hiding from Morocco and was home before the postcards; the other won the tournament.

Maybe the significant difference between Scotland and France is that we are not a multi-cultural society. The French team's best players were drawn from France's immigrant communities. Desailly and Thuram hail from West Africa, and the mad monk, Zinedine Zidane, is from France's most troublesome former colony, Algeria.

It took the World Cup to bring France to its senses. Despite the tensions that poverty and racism can bring, new immigrants are always, in the final instance, net contributors to a culture. They bring dreams and determination that add value to the country they settle in. To begin with you get a couple of new restaurants but if you get lucky, they chuck in a half-decent midfield player into the bargain.

New immigrants are always, in the final instance, net contributors

It is a pity Scottish football has not benefited from large-scale immigration. Some will point to Irish immigrants in the last century and the role they played in the foundation of Celtic, Hibs and Dundee United. But that was a long time ago and whatever energies came with Irish immigrants as they escaped famine have long since been absorbed into the mainstream of our society.

There will be others who will point to the influx of Italians after the war. A few players – including Marinello and Macari – trickled into the system. But Italians came in small numbers. Rangers bought more Italians over the last four seasons than emerged through the ranks of the Scottish schools system from over 50 years of migration.

Compare Scotland's low-key social history to Holland, where football has been re-written by second-generation immigrants from Surinam. Gullit, Rijkaard, Seedorf, Kluivert and Davids would be in most people's dream team. You could even pick Regi Blinker to carry the hamper and Bobby Petta to tip the doorman.

By comparison, it is only two years ago that Scotland capped Kevin Harper, its first black footballer, and most fans would struggle to name a single indigenous black player in senior Scottish football. Promisingly, but again in isolation, St Johnstone have the impressively-named Emmanuel Panther, an African Scot who has been capped at schoolboy level, in their youth academy. But it's thin pickings.

The source of Scotland's under-performance at international level is frequently blamed on poor youth development. Maybe we should add to that the absence of an immigrant culture that has impacted on our football heritage.

It has been more than 50 years since the SS Emperor Windrush brought the first Jamaican immigrants to Britain. I suppose you've already gathered that it didn't dock in Greenock. At the time Scotland was a relatively poor country with high unemployment and no real job opportunities. Scots eagerly took any low-paid jobs that were available. Down south, there was a labour shortage. Health and transport officials were dispatched to the Caribbean to recruit West Indian immigrants in order to work in London's hospitals or in public transport in Leeds and Birmingham.

Fifty years on the grandchildren of those West Indian immigrants – players such as Sol Campbell – are proud to wear England strips. If only the SS Emperor Windrush had run aground on the beach at Largs, then maybe some of England's new black footballers would have been born in Scotland.

France's victory in the 1998 World Cup final ushered in a new multi-cultural era for football. The future belongs to those teams who can draw on a rich tapestry of new talent. It is a shame that Scotland's recent history has made our rug so threadbare.

13

THE UNHOLY TRINITY

Suddenly, the heavens fell in. After years of prevarication, God finally came out of the closet and admitted he's a Protestant.

On Monday 10 July 1989, the whole of Scotland played judge and jury. Maurice Johnston, a red-haired Glaswegian in his mid-twenties, appeared before flashing news cameras. With a few faltering words he admitted his part in Glasgow's most heinous incident.

"Rangers are a great club and I'm glad to have joined them," Johnston said, turning a button on his coat, if not the entire coat itself.

On that day, a disbelieving nation began to come to terms with the realisation that a tradition stretching back all but 116 years had finally been broken. Glasgow Rangers, the last great bastion of Scottish Protestantism, had finally signed a high-profile Catholic.

When Johnston's transfer was announced, every other news story paled into insignificance. Genocide in China, crises in the food industry, a rail strike, cabinet disagreement about the European monetary system. They all faded into insignificance. Glasgow Rangers had signed a bead-rattler.

In the Eighties Maurice Johnston was one of an unholy trinity of players whose lives caught the popular imagination of the increasingly sensationalist tabloid press. The other two were an unemployed dustman from Milton, Frank McAvennie, and a young football prodigy who smashed Scotland's seasonal goalscoring record famously winning a jeroboam of bubbly from the *Daily Record*. His name was 'Champagne Charlie' Nicholas.

For more than a decade their careers inter-weaved and their personal lives invariably found their way into the daily gossip columns. It sometimes seems that they were vying for attention, or trying to upstage each other in the quest to find Scotland's undisputed bad boy.

On the 10th of July 1989 Maurice Johnston won on points.

Ironically, the sectarian clamour that greeted Johnston's move to Rangers went against the grain of Scotland's political self-development. In almost every walk of civic society there was a desire to break from the past and mould a Scotland that was outward looking, and could leave the luggage of the parochial past behind.

Scotland was trying to establish its credentials as a modern, independent

Right, repeat after me: "The cry… was… no… surrender…"

and progressive nation; surely such a primitive obsession with religion and sport was an incriminating liability?

Did the mask slip? Was the country that spent most of the Thatcher years claiming the moral high ground just a little backwater? You bet your sister's confirmation dress it was.

Strictly speaking, Mo Johnston was not the first Catholic to sign for Rangers, but he was easily the most famous. Others before him had either escaped through the net or simply married into what Ibrox orthodoxy thought was the wrong family.

Johnston was born in Springburn in Glasgow's East End, the son of a Catholic mother and Protestant father. Nicknamed Mojo, he grew up a die-hard Celtic fan and to those who are familiar with the lumbering tribalism

Rangers had not simply signed a Catholic, they had plucked the biggest green grape in the vineyard

of Scottish football, he was easily identified with the Catholic side of soccer's religious psyche.

Rangers had not simply signed a Catholic, they had plucked the biggest green grape in the vineyard.

As soon as the news of Johnston's transfer was announced to the press, all hell broke out. Loyal Protestants burned Rangers scarves and vowed never to return to Ibrox, staunch Catholics made him Public Enemy Number One for promising to re-sign for Celtic then spurning them at the eleventh hour. Effigies of the Rangers manager Graeme Souness were burned in Belfast. Overnight graffiti magically appeared on the streets of Glasgow's East End. Each crudely sprayed slogan was a testimony to warped faith: "Mo Surrender", "Wanted Dead Or Alive

Laying a wreath for the ghost of Rangers' past

Maurice Johnston The Turncoat", "Souness You Roman Bastard" and in a more chilling reminder of IRA discipline, a piece of graffiti at Glasgow's Bellgrove Station threateningly warned that "Collaborators Can't Play Without Kneecaps". Wreaths were ceremoniously laid at Ibrox as fans mourned the death of institutional Protestantism.

A screen of strict security was thrown up around Johnston and his immediate family. Officials of Rangers hinted he was already in hiding and may be forced to stay in London flying to Ibrox by secret charter flight every morning for training.

A small, quixotic and easily provoked player, the ginger-haired Johnston and his contemporaries Nicholas and McAvennie were more accustomed to that other unholy trinity: goals, nightclubs and Page Three girls.

The very thought that a religious fatwah could descend on Scotland was in every respect bizarre. Whatever they say now, Souness, Johnston and his infamous agent Bill McMurdo seriously underestimated the anger his transfer would unleash.

The backdrop to Johnston's move to Rangers was also more complex than most fans now remember. It took place at the height of the marching season. The previous week, six Scots had been sentenced to a total of 64 years in jail for running illegal arms operations for the UDA from public houses in Perth. Inevitably, they were Rangers fans, which allowed investigative newspapers to speculate that Rangers supporters' buses travelling every week from Belfast to Scotland were used for the trafficking of sectarian and paramilitary business.

O come all ye faithful

The Mo Johnston saga, with its undercurrent of sacrilege and deceit, highlighted a phenomenon that only the Irish and the Scots can fully appreciate. It is a mood or attitude that is absent from official news coverage of sectarianism and is perhaps best described as the 'pleasures of bigotry' or – put more simply – the funny side of being a Fenian.

News coverage of the troubles in Ireland and the religious divisions that exist in Belfast, Derry and Glasgow are usually represented in a serious and censorious light. A discourse of worried dismay has settled over the way sectarianism is covered. But in the communities themselves a very different attitude is at play. Bigotry and belly laughs often live side by side, and The Mojo Story is by far the most public example of sectarian farce.

Despite the animosity between Rangers and Celtic and the acts of sporadic violence that often accompanied Old Firm matches, the Mojo transfer wars were accompanied by humour. Jokes acted as a safety valve, which tended to keep the heat of sectarianism at an acceptable temperature. The tabloid press had a field day. Here was an open invitation to indulge in two of the cardinal virtues of popular journalism: humour and scaremongering. Jokes exploded like Semtex. Apparently, on the night Johnston signed for Rangers, a Catholic woman had quads at Glasgow's Southern General Hospital; the irate father decided to call them Eenie, Meenie, Minie and Pat. Within hours of his transfer, the Mojo joke had arrived in earnest. No wonder he had problems with his Celtic contract – he couldn't read Latin.

The *Daily Record* led the pack, proudly announcing an exclusive under the memorable headline "Death Threat To A Dog Named Mo". This was

On the night Johnston signed for Rangers, a Catholic woman had quads at Glasgow's Southern General; the irate father decided to call them Eenie, Meenie, Minie and Pat

the sad story of Mrs Nan O'Malley of Dumbarton and her hapless five-year-old mongrel Mo. The dog had been threatened with death by local psychos for daring to share its name with Maurice Johnston. "What kind of mentality do people have?" asked the bewildered housewife, unaware that a few miles away in deepest Dalmarnock, the local polis believed that a more dastardly plot was being hatched.

The assassination theory

The case of Peter Lees and Peter Fitzgerald remains one of the most bizarre and unexplained incidents in the Mo Johnston controversy. Ardent Celtic fans since birth, the two men were detained in police custody under Section 2 of the Criminal Justice Act on 26 August 1989, the day of the Old Firm match. Although they were released without charge, rumours circulated in Glasgow that two men were plotting to assassinate Johnston, who was playing his first game for Rangers against Celtic.

The rumour gathered momentum when it was revealed that Lees had stood trial along with five others in 1984 accused of the murder of an Irishman, James McCollum of Donegal. Lees had been acquitted of all charges. His involvement in the trial was enough to heat up a cauldron of exaggeration. But in the heat of Mojo mania, the press, the police and the public put two and two together and came up with the arithmetical answer – 1690. Was Lees an IRA hitman? Definitely not – he was acquitted of all charges, and ultimately sued the police for wrongful arrest. Lees was simply a Celtic fan who, in the words of one die-hard Tim, believed that "Judas should be nailed to the cross."

Like his two amigos Frank McAvennie and Charlie Nicholas, Johnston has never been backward at

coming forward. He is easily the most public anti-hero in the history of Scottish football. Although death threats and demonstrations forced him into temporary isolation in Graeme Souness's luxury home near Edinburgh, it was obvious that Mojo would not be out of the headlines for long.

On 1 November 1989, in mid-season, the inevitable happened. "Mo Stuns Them By Singing The Sash", screamed a headline in the *Daily Record*. By the end of the season, The Govan True Blues – a supporters' club not normally known to surrender and compromise – had voted Johnston player of the year.

Catching prominent football personalities in sectarianism's answer to *in flagrante* is a favourite device of popular journalism. The Rangers vice-chairman Donald Findlay was forced to resign when a shabby home video recorded him singing 'The Sash' at a supporter's club on the night Rangers won the Scottish Cup. And like an innocent abroad, the Dutch internationalist Ronald De Boer was duped into having his photograph taken with the UDA killer Michael Stone. The photo was front page news in the *Sunday Mail* but everyone knew De Boer didn't have a clue who the skulker beside him really was.

If secret photographs are the bane of the Scottish footballer's life, champagne is their reward. The poor man's cocaine has always been a companion in the lives of successful Scottish stars, not least the unholy trinity.

Back in 1984, Maurice Johnston was the star of a Watford team which had unexpectedly grafted its way to the FA Cup final at Wembley. Although they lost, the club's flamboyant chairman Elton John threw a party to console his beaten troops. As the champagne flowed, the pop star performed an impromptu solo concert, dedicating

Shedding a tear for sectarianism

his greatest hits to members of the Watford team. When it came to singing *Candle in the Wind*, there was only one serious contender, a flame-haired striker from Glasgow:

They seem to think he lives his life
Like a scandal in the wind
Never knowing who to cling to
When the rain sets in.

The dodgy tracksuit

Football players are frequently sucked into scandals that are in every sense mundane. Long before Mojo signed for Rangers, he was already one of Scottish football's most notorious players. In his days as a Celt, rumour chased Johnston like a frantic full-back. He spent time in jail and was on the receiving end of a paternity suit, which haunted him from christening to courtroom.

And then there were the dodgy tracksuits.

In 1985, soon after he had left Watford to join Celtic, Johnston was found guilty of resetting three track-suits worth a total of £85. Stipendiary Magistrate Robert Hamilton fined him £200 and the court heard how Police Sergeant William Donaldson had apprehended four men acting furtive-ly in a doorway near a sports shop in Glasgow's Mitchell Street. The track-suits had been hi-jacked from the shop and the bold Mo had been caught in mid-bargain.

The case of the wandering tracksuits does not end with Johnston's folly. Nor does it end with the judge's summing up – "I could really make a name for myself and lock you up." It ends with the wisdom of Celtic manager Davie Hay who defended the honour of his club. In a statement that captures the calamitous short-sightedness that has long been Celtic's hallmark, Hay brushed off the incident, "It was some-thing which happened while Johnston was with another team. It wouldn't happen while he was with Celtic."

Too true, when Mo pulled on the green and white big-time trouble was sure to follow.

On Tuesday 17 March, 1987 at Glasgow Sheriff Court, George Lynch and Maurice Johnston were found guilty of assault on the premises of the 'Mardi Gras', a popular nightspot in Dunlop Street, Glasgow's Disco Alley. Lynch, described as Mo's minder in the press, was fined £250 and the luckless Johnston was fined £500 for attacking a local youth Scott Leslie and fracturing his jaw.

Johnston along with his team mate Alan

'Rambo' McInally had been invited into the club by the management. A private party was in full swing. Kevin McGrory, a Celtic fan, described the victim as being "blootered drunk". A fracas ensued in which the court determined that Lynch headbutted the youth and Johnston punched him with such force he fractured Leslie's jaw and had to have his own hand set in plaster. Despite his reputation for charging in where angels fear to tread, McInally faded into the background and was not in court to see the irrepressible Johnston sign autographs for a group of teenage girls.

Mince pie diplomacy

To reduce Johnston's off-field career to sectarian scandal and nightclub brawls does him a massive injustice. His quixotic skills took him to France, where a successful career with FC Nantes and a pan-European friend-ship with the Belgian international Frankie Vercauteren turned Mo from football's typical Glasgow fly-boy into an accomplished European player.

It was fitting that Mo's next brush with the law would be in a suitably European ambience, namely Gordon's Italian Trattoria on Edinburgh's Royal Mile.

According to court dispatches, a brawl in the Trattoria led to two of Johnston's associates being fined for assaulting the restaurateur Mr Remo Maciocia. Johnston was called to give evidence. He resolutely denied shout-ing, "Put the head on him" and took no part in a reported incident where one of the accused dropped his draw-ers and "mooned" at the Trattoria's guests. In cross-examination, Johnston admitted his past crimes but adamant-ly assured the court he was "an honest man".

Only the most cynical bystander could doubt his words; the incident happened after Scotland's most famous footballer had spent months

In cross-examination, Johnston admitted his past crimes but adamantly assured the court he was "an honest man"

living in virtual quarantine, hounded by the press and isolated by his country's appetite for sectarianism. His family had been threatened, he had been the victim of a failed arson attempt and he was a sitting duck if he dared to walk the streets of Glasgow again.

Poor Mo, even the wrath of one of Glasgow's greatest institutions – the half-time pie – was to fall on his head.

On November 4 1989, at Ibrox during an emotional league match with his old club Celtic, Johnston was assaulted with a pie. The accused, Ronald Taylor of Glenrothes, denied committing a breach of the peace at Rangers Broomloan Stand and rejected the claim that he hit Johnston on the back of the head with a half-eaten pie.

Pie throwing has a long and hon-ourable tradition in Scottish football. In the modern era, in which bottles and cans have been banned from sen-ior grounds, until it was upstaged by the pound coin, the pie was the Rolls Royce of missiles – a football fan who has not witnessed crusted pastry in full flight has lived a sheltered life. Perhaps the cruellest incidence of mince pie diplomacy took place at Easter Road during a league match between Hibs and Celtic. In an act of extreme provocation, a pie was aimed at Celtic's Danny McGrain, a diabetic who was scrupulously careful about his diet.

Don't call me scarface

From the day he signed for Rangers, Mo Johnston was hunted high and low by the tabloid press. At times he seemed to attract notoriety like a magnet and at times he was the unfortunate victim of media skullduggery.

Maurice Johnston is as much a product of tabloid journalism as its victim. Throughout his career, his agent and financial minder Bill McMurdo has gone to great lengths to cultivate an interest in the player, often speaking openly to the press, encouraging a high public profile and using the media to enhance the player's celebrity status.

The 1990 World Cup, with its "Scots Stars in Champagne Booze-up" headlines, marked a fresh low point in the relations between Johnston and the press. As Scotland returned home defeated again, for the fans it meant the obligatory period of soul searching and for Mo Johnston the return trip home meant the apparent end of his international career.

Predictability has never been Maurice's forte. The dust had settled on another ill-fated campaign when the controversial striker announced he would never play for Scotland again. Despite heavy counselling from Graeme Souness, he was absent when Scotland embarked on their European Nation's Cup campaign at home against the much-fancied Romanians. The small but noisy crowd that watched Scotland win by the odd goal

The press have it in for Mo again

chanted in derision throughout the game. Johnston had not only turned his back on Celtic, now it seemed he had rejected Scotland as well.

Johnston's explanation for withdrawing from the international scene – putting club before country – fell on stony ground when he was sent home in disgrace from Rangers' pre-season training session in the late summer of

1990. Exhilarated by his championship success and insistent that an Italian style of preparation would be instilled in his players, Graeme Souness took Rangers to the hills of Tuscany. Discipline was on a hiding to nothing.

According to dispatches, Johnston was involved in an unseemly late night incident, drank too much, and according to official explanations fell and smashed his face on the bed springs. Once again the press had a field day, but this time Johnston's patience with the press was stretched too far and he took out court injunctions against two English newspapers claiming that their reporting of the dispute with Souness had been defamatory.

At its most critical stage, the incident threatened to end Johnston's spectacular career at Rangers. Most commentators thought Souness's increasingly disciplinarian mood would end in Johnston's abject departure from Ibrox – but a contrite apology saved Johnston's skin.

Johnston stayed at Ibrox to fight another day. As unexpectedly as he had announced the end of his international career, Johnston did another monumental u-turn. Spurred on by a patriotic mother and promising to donate his Scotland fees to charity, the unpredictable Mo joined the Hampden circus again.

After periods at Hearts and Falkirk, Johnston moved to safer waters across the Atlantic and he is alive and well and still playing professionally in Kansas. Despite persistent rumours, however, Johnston has never shared a flat with Salman Rushdie.

Short-sleeved cardigan meets big girls' blouse

There's a guy down the chip shop swears he's Charlie

Charlie Nicholas – part two of the unholy trinity – is a one-man morality tale. His career lurched from one extreme to another, noisy then quiet, a prolific goalscorer then a famine victim, a superstar then a substitute. Worst of all, a player and then a pundit.

To the football fans who have followed his exploits Nicholas is 'Champagne Charlie', the John Travolta of Scotland and the uncrowned king of the late licence. But when the chips are down and like the

rest of the unholy trinity, he has been a victim of his public image.

Charlie was raised in Glasgow's Maryhill, where the Jags hailed, the Mental Fleet sailed and the neighbourhood had an obsession with football. Raised on the Wyndford housing scheme, where he lived next door to the Celtic, Dundee and Partick Thistle player Jim Duffy, Nicholas was a pupil at St Columba of Iona, a local Catholic school.

"I hated school," he claims. "Getting a game of football on a Saturday for

the school team was great. I enjoyed P.E. except for odd occasions in the winter when we had to go into the gym and dance with the birds," he once said. By the time he was 20 and the most prodigiously gifted Celtic player of his generation, Charlie had discovered that dancing with the birds had its own special charm.

After a long apprenticeship with Celtic Boys Club, playing as a winger then a defensive sweeper, Nicholas attracted the attention of several English league teams and was invited to trials at Ipswich, Wolves and Manchester City. It was the Ipswich setup under the management of Bobby Robson which most impressed him and the East Anglian team offered the teenager £4,000 to sign. Unfortunately, they played in blue strips and Celtic fans would later claim Nicholas could not face the prospect of signing for a team that wore the same colour of shirts as Rangers, instead returning to Celtic Boys Club to await his calling from Paradise.

Celtic is an institution that periodically has been run as destitution. It began as a charity team for Irish immigrants in Glasgow's East End in 1888 and won the European Cup in 1967. But between those years – and for most of the time since – it has resented spending money. According to myth, the Celtic funds are kept in a miserly biscuit tin, a closely guarded money chest under the Parkhead bed. Critics often dismissed Celtic as a club that has taken its roots in poverty and charity to extremes.

Charlie Nicholas was no exception. By December 1982, when Celtic lifted the League Cup for the first time since the mid-Seventies, Nicholas had established himself as the young sensation of Scottish football. In one remarkable season he scored 51 goals, became the undisputed Player of the Year, and dispelled the illusion that the former Celtic hero Kenny Dalglish would never be replaced. His goal-scoring prowess won him Scotland's Golden

"I promise to do Scotland proud and waste as much time as I can in nightclubs"

Boot Award, a magnum of Moet Chandon and the nickname 'Champagne Charlie'. But at the height of Charlie's love affair with Celtic the romance turned sour when he rejected an "insulting" financial offer from the Celtic board.

It was with a feeling of animosity that Nicholas accepted an offer from London and was transferred to Arsenal for £750,000. "It's a sad fact that Celtic have taken advantage of their top players," he claimed in his ghostwritten biography, "The kind of players who have supported Celtic and been really loyal to the club have been the ones who have suffered the most." This image of Celtic was one that dated back to the 1920s when the club tried to sell the free-scoring centre-forward Jimmy McGrory when he was

Johnston had not only turned his back on Celtic, now it seemed he had rejected Scotland as well

en route to a pilgrimage at Lourdes. But if Nicholas felt he had suffered at the hands of Celtic, then the suffering he experienced in London at the hands of the media was to force him out of the limelight and into a melancholic shell.

Champagne Charlie's move to London was a tactical disaster. Although he had a choice of several clubs, including Liverpool, Manchester United and Inter Milan, Nicholas unadvisedly chose London.

Nicholas was not the first Scottish star to make the error of moving to London in the belief that the terraces are paved with gold. Hughie Gallacher moved to Chelsea in the '30s. Peter Marinello transferred from Hibs to Arsenal in the '60s. And the third member of the unholy trinity, Frank McAvennie, moved to West Ham. The Soho night seems to enchant high-living Scots.

Critics of his move to Arsenal, including Graeme Souness, claimed he was putting his social life, his image and his pop marketability before football. Charlie denied it. Charlie would. But the warning failed to prevent a catastrophic decline in his football fortunes.

Cheque-point Charlie

At Centre Point, the Soho reception centre for runaways, where social workers advise young Scots to avoid the pitfalls of drug abuse, sex offenders and amusement arcades, there is no-one to advise footballers. And no-one had the foresight to tell Charlie Nicholas, the young Glaswegian in a white leather suit, about a species infinitely more troublesome than rentboy racketeers: cockney football agents with their eye on the main chance.

In his first season at Arsenal Nicholas was cast in the role of footballer turned male model. Although he endeared himself to Arsenal's North Bank and played impressively enough on the outskirts of the box to sustain his reputation for skilful adventure, he rarely found the net at Highbury and began to look like over-paid hype to the public.

At his most impressionable, Nicholas allowed himself to be talked into publicity stunts that horribly backfired. He appeared on stage at Wembley as part of a Tory rally in support of Margaret Thatcher. The move apparently upset his father – a redundant trade unionist – and provoked derision in the anti-Thatcher heartland of central Scotland, where Nicholas was caricatured as a dupe.

As goals at Arsenal became fewer, most people plumped for the most obvious explanation; Nicholas was a victim of the magical trio – bevvy, birds and big-heads. The evidence seems overwhelming. There was Stringfellows' nightclub, the friendship with an aerobic gymnast, newspaper photos of him stripped to the waist, the gold earrings, and his nights on the town.

Teresa Bazar of the pop group Dollar remembered her night with Nicholas and it seemed to capture the predicament to a tee. Her thoughts on the champagne kid were recorded for posterity in *The Book of Football Quotations.* "We talked about football but all he wanted to talk about was sex," she said, before adding, "I hear he's not been scoring many goals recently and that's why he left Arsenal, but all I can tell you is he

Champagne Charlie tests a bed

certainly scored a hat-trick with me that night."

Holiday in hell

Charlie's reputation was increasingly dogged by misfortune. When he least needed the attention of a photographer one was sure to be on call. When he most needed a month of solitude away from screaming headlines, something from his past was inevitably dug up. If scandal was the sorcerer, Charlie was its reliable apprentice. He once summed up his own fate by saying, "If I go into a bar and have a lager shandy, word goes back that I'm knocking back bottles of champagne. By the time it gets to the papers or my manager at Arsenal, it's me lying in the gutter."

Haunted by an over-imaginative press, Charlie Nicholas was to confront his worst ordeal in September 1986 in what can only be described as the case of the stolen chip. It was a bizarre affair which shows how events can entrap a famous footballer. The incident took place when Charlie and his long-time friend and fellow Celtic Boys' Club colleague Willie McStay were on holiday together in Ibiza. In what seemed like an innocuous joke, N i c h o l a s allegedly tried to steal a chip from a holi-d a y m a k e r outside the Confusion Bar in San Antonio, Ibiza. The rest is her story.

Charlie hides his Sky
TV microphone
under his towel

And the nominations are ... Robert di Niro for *Charlie*

At the time her chip was stolen Lori McElroy, a latter-day *femme fatale* from East Kilbride, was 28 and enjoying a holiday abroad with her student boyfriend. Westminster County Court, where the incident washed up, heard that an argument had ensued and that Nicholas reputedly slapped and punched the girl, fracturing her jaw. Judge McDonnel dismissed the attack as "an arrogant and cowardly assault" and scolded Nicholas by saying, "I am old-fashioned enough to think it is particularly nasty for a man to strike a woman, especially an athletic man."

To this day the truth of what happened is shrouded in mystery. Nicholas still protests his innocence while readily admitting to other misdemeanours. He denies that the exchange was anything like as bad as the court supposed and although he paid £1,300 damages to the victim, he is adamant that an injustice was done. According to his solicitor at the time Nicholas was "bitterly disappointed with the verdict because he is not a violent man". Unfortunately the newspapers printed a different version.

According to press reports at the time, McElroy and her boyfriend claimed Nicholas and his friends had been a problem throughout the holiday. "During the holiday we saw Nicholas more than once," she told the *Daily Mail*. "He was always acting flash, wearing white leather suits and drinking champagne. He seemed to think he should have a lot of attention."

Brown claimed he was guilty of the assault, adding implausibly that Charlie was "pure as the driven snow"

But trouble flared when the chip was stolen. McElroy apparently shouted, "Listen Charlie we're not impressed so go off and pester someone else." The court heard that Nicholas then turned violent. "At that Mr Nicholas slapped my face hard then gave me a solid punch to the jaw," McElroy claimed.

The evidence swung in an unexpected direction when Nicholas called a witness in his defence, a friend Christopher Brown, who was also on holiday in Ibiza. Brown claimed he, not Nicholas, was guilty of the assault, adding implausibly that Charlie was "pure as the driven snow". As an audible ripple of laughter went round the courtroom Brown denied vehemently that he had been "set up to take the rap for the footballer".

It was Charlie's worst nightmare. He had to go through the public humiliation of denying he had a drink problem and retreated from the court saying, "I've been found guilty so there's nothing anyone can do. But in my heart I still know I'm innocent."

Home is where the heart is

The following month the legal process smiled more kindly on Charlie

"Don't take a photo now – I haven't finished the decorating yet"

Nicholas when a three year drink driving ban was shortened by a year allowing him to buy a new £11,000 Porsche. But in the world of football, the word was out, yet another Scottish player had been tarnished with an uncontrollable image.

In October 1987, when his days at Arsenal were numbered, a £600,000 transfer to FC Toulon was almost in place when the French club made an unprecedented contractual demand, a morality clause, which would guarantee the player's good behaviour. The transfer fell through and Charlie returned to the Scottish Premier League to play for Aberdeen.

Charlie Nicholas had left his mark on English football as one of the great imponderables, a player of exquisite skill, an under-achiever, a player literally troubled by the burden of being brilliant.

One of the most sobering institutions in Hampden Babylon is marriage. For Charlie Nicholas his betrothal to his wife Claire and the cosier prospect of a future as a father was apparently a watershed in his development. Despite an incident in Aberdeen in 1989 when he was reported to the Procurator Fiscal for what the law delicately describes as "a public nuisance offence", Nicholas rebuilt his

Lori McElroy's chips were stolen

reputation. After all, Aberdeen's heritage was built on fish and it still has the highest concentration of chip shops in Scotland.

It came as no surprise in 1990 when Nicholas returned home to Parkhead. His former Arsenal team mate Martin Hayes and the ex-Hibernian midfield player John Collins joined too. When Nicholas returned to Parkhead to play his home debut in a showpiece friendly against Everton he was greeted with rapturous applause.

Ironically, in his biography, written soon after his move to Arsenal, Charlie Nicholas had vowed he would never darken Celtic's door again. "Since I left, there has been talk about my going back to Celtic, but that will never happen." Inevitably it did.

But by now the magic was on the wane. A future next to Jim White in the Sky TV studios awaited the tongue-tied Charlie Nicholas. It was only then that Scottish football fans learned the truth. Torn ligaments and thigh strains may have been inflicted throughout his career but the affliction that most conspired against Charlie Nicholas was grammar.

To this day he suffers from an acute case of irritable vowel syndrome.

Frank's wild years

Let us not pay homage to the unholy trinity without another mention of the cathedral they prayed in – Stringfellows.

If the management of London's premier 1980s nightclub was to take its snobbish door-policy to its ultimate conclusion and investigate the social backgrounds of their glittering clientele, at least one regular would be out on his ear.

Frances McAvennie, a former council roadsweeper from Glasgow's Milton housing scheme, is not the kind of character you would have immediately associated with the glamorous lifestyle.

But football bestows incredible social status on those with skill.

In his wildest years Frank McAvennie, a sweeper turned striker, managed to overcome his humble origins, dye his hair blond and become one of London's disco glitterati. His peroxide reign has made him one of the most recognisable anti-heroes in Scottish football. To this day he is one of the most love-able stereotypes in Scotland, forever imprisoned by Jonathan Watson's unnerving impersonation, and the catchphrase "Where's The Burdz?"

Into the twilight zone

It all began in a more humble way. After a successful infancy with the junior side Johnstone Burgh, McAvennie was spotted by manager Jim Clunie and signed to St Mirren, the enterprising Paisley side whose ability to discover talent at the time was matched only by their pressure to sell them to bigger clubs.

After an inauspicious start to his career, in which he fractured his skull in a clash with Dundee United's David Narey, Frank became a firm favourite at Love Street. His skills were allied to a questionable temperament, and in January 1985 Frank McAvennie lived up to his immense promise, becoming the first Scottish footballer to be sent off in a Premier League match for giving a 'V' sign to opposing fans. The Hearts supporters in question, no

"Give us a kiss, Ginger"

strangers to rudeness themselves, immediately christened him 'Frank The Wank' and McAvennie's controversial future was secured.

By June 1985, he was established as one of Scottish football's most persistent goalscorers and left St Mirren, with a £340,000 transfer taking him south to West Ham. Unlike many expensive Scottish signings who had preceeded him, McAvennie took to English football like a gin to tonic. In his first season he became the uncrowned King of the East End, scoring 28 goals and setting up an unrivalled scoring partnership with Tony Cottee.

McAvennie's goals were free tickets to every nightclub in London and despite a quiet off-field life when he first moved to London, he finally succumbed to temptation and took his rightful place in the twilight zone.

At a footballer's dinner in Glasgow, the former Celtic manager Liam Brady once joked that team mates nicknamed Macca 'Ginger-Pubes', adding with glee, "I can assure you Frank's blonde hair isn't natural."

But the bottle blonde managed to fool the damsels of the night. Never in the history of human seduction has one man given so much attention to the cause of international womanhood as the man from Milton. While the rest of Scotland's football antiheroes stumbled from one seedy den to another, drinking anything in their way, Frank McAvennie has devoted his life to human affection. In the words of one over-excited Fleet Street commentator, "his tipple is nipple".

Keeping abreast of things

McAvennie's penchant for the pectoral glands began in earnest when he joined West Ham. His brief relationship with a Page Three girl Julie Desmond hit the skids when the press revealed that the bold Frank was two-timing her for another model, Anita Blue. In a frivolous but fascinating series of articles in the English tabloids, the scorned woman described him as "Ratavennie", saying his "tactics were firmly offside".

Over a period of nearly two years, when he was involved with the two models, McAvennie had his sights on Jenny Blyth, one of the *Daily Star*'s highest paid models and an undisputed star among Page Three girls. When their paths crossed at parties, McAvennie used all his charm to convince her that workies from Glasgow were the best lovers. It worked. Fearless Frank phoned her on a regular basis and left messages with her unsuspecting boyfriend, a West Ham fan who was pleased that the team's top scorer was training so late at night.

In October 1987 McAvennie returned to Scotland, signing for Celtic for £725,000. By this time his brief engagement to Blue had ended and his pursuit of Jenny Blyth was paying dividends. Their relationship was made in tabloid heaven. One of Scotland's richest footballers and one of Britain's most marketable models were an item and according to a highly quotable "close friend", who in true tabloid style was never named, Frank was supposedly "besotted" by the blonde lovely.

But back in Glasgow there was another matter to deal with – trouble.

Hearts supporters immediately christened McAvennie 'Frank The Wank'

"I played with much bigger tits at St Mirren"

Go directly to jail

Inspector James Moir of Strathclyde Police submitted his report in a style that reflects the matter-of-fact grammar of a cop in charge of a pen:

"About 3.15 pm as I was patrolling near the west end of the stadium, my attention was attracted to an incident near the Rangers goal-mouth," wrote the observant Inspector. "I saw that the Rangers goal-keeper Christopher Woods had come out of his goal and had been challenged by the Celtic player Francis McAvennie. I saw McAvennie quite deliberately strike

In the words of one over-excited Fleet Street commentator, "his tipple is nipple"

the Rangers keeper Woods with what I would describe as a slap on the face. The Rangers keeper in turn seemed to put his right forearm against McAvennie's face and push him away. The next thing was the Rangers centre-half, Butcher joined the other two and they then began to jostle each other."

As the temperature approached boiling point, Inspector Moir proceeded in a westerly direction. "I was then aware of the Rangers football player Graham Roberts running across from the opposite side of the park," he continued. "I then saw him quite deliberately punch the Celtic player McAvennie on the side of the head, causing McAvennie to fall to the ground. The whole attitude of the

crowd was very volatile and it seemed to me that we were in great danger of a pitch invasion."

The battle of '87 took place against a background of profound change in Scottish football. Although the drama was played out in the familiar costumes of the blue and the green, three of the performers were English internationals, new to the ferocious emotionalism of the Scottish game and naïve in their understanding of the religious sub-cultures of sectarianism.

The arrival of big-name signings from England was a cornerstone of Graeme Souness's attempts to dismantle the primitive traditionalism at Ibrox and build Rangers into a progressive force in European football.

Like every other visionary in the Scottish game, Souness under-estimated Scotland's love affair with the limitations of the past. His idea of the future was a super-league contest against Inter Milan in the San Siro, but most fans who prayed at his feet got their fix from seeing a nasty wee squabble with Celtic at the arse end of the Copeland Road. Saturday 17 October 1987 was one of those days.

The Procurator Fiscal, Sandy Jessop, was made aware that the match had bordered on lawlessness. Butcher, Woods, Roberts and McAvennie were summoned to Govan police station and charged with "conduct likely to provoke a breach of the peace amongst spectators". As parlance would have it: the Old Firm had been 'lifted'.

Quite apart from the central charges, the Procurator Fiscal itemised other incidents to be taken into consideration. In the first, well before the fight took place, McAvennie had "recklessly bundled Woods into the net", but the other two incidents had the more serious connotations. At a critical moment in the game, Peter Grant celebrated a Celtic goal by mak-

What do you call a guy from Milton in a suit? The defendant

ing the Catholic sign of the cross and in response, Graham Roberts, who replaced Woods in goal, "conducted" the Rangers support in a noisy rendition of 'The Sash'. In a drama unprecedented in Scottish football, a group of players – either by direct accusation or by association – were implicated in a sectarian farce, which could have ended in serious public disorder.

East End boys, West End girls

At the height of his fame in Scotland,

'Til death us do part

The rumpus led to comments that McAvennie had passed his prime. In football maybe, but scandal – never

McAvennie flew to London as a member of the Scotland squad that lost to England at Wembley in 1988. As the Tartan Army drowned its sorrows in the bars of Soho, Frank preferred a candlelit dinner. "We really hit it off," said Jenny. "The more champagne I drank the better I understood his strong Scottish accent. I'd barely finished my prawn cocktail before I realised I could fall for him."

Entranced by the aphrodisiacs in his own cocktail, McAvennie began to visit his new girl every weekend, flying to the London nightlife and eventually provoking a dispute with Celtic manager Billy McNeill when he failed to show up for a Monday morning training session. He proposed on Valentine's Day 1989.

It was the beginning of his life with Jenny Blyth and the end of his lifelong love affair with Celtic. Booed off the pitch in his last game for the club, he joined West Ham and left Glasgow chanting a familiar mantra. "Playing for Celtic has curtailed my freedom. There are some places I just can't go to." The places Frank McAvennie had in mind opened at 10pm and had flashing light shows and enamel ice buckets on legs.

McAvennie's second spell at West Ham was in marked contrast to his first. Although he bought Jenny a £2,000 diamond engagement ring and happily re-settled in his Brentford mansion, his scoring prowess deserted him after a vicious tackle by Stoke's Chris Kamara left McAvennie with a broken leg. It was an injury that kept

him out of first team football for months and has left him with a limp to this day.

In January 1990, the month his home city wore the prestigious crown of European Capital of Culture, Frankie Mac from deepest Milton celebrated in his own uniquely cultured way. With Jenny Blyth nowhere to be found – vindictive press reports claiming that the marriage of the decade was on the rocks – he became embroiled in an unseemly dispute with his own club. This time the venue was an upmarket hotel in Hornchurch, Essex.

According to reports, McAvennie and a couple of unnamed cohorts left the club's Christmas dinner and tried to gate-crash a private party being held in the hotel by West Ham's commercial manager Brian Blower. A hotel insider told the *Sun*, "Mr Blower just wanted a quiet family party and when he told McAvennie he couldn't get in there was a lot of pushing and shoving."

Blower's account of the incident was considerably more revealing. He alleged that a West Ham player assaulted him, in front of his wife, telling the *Daily Express*, "What happened totally ruined it, punches were thrown." Angered by the incident, he demanded a written apology and then threatened to take a writ out against McAvennie.

The Christmas rumpus led to comments that Frank McAvennie had passed his prime. In terms of football maybe, but scandal – never.

Carry on misbehaving

McAvennie's subsequent life has been a rake's progress. At the height of the property boom, he made an ill-advised investment in a mock Tudor mansion and the market collapsed, leaving McAvennie with debts. He has since been charged with drugs offences, been involved in several

The saddest thing of all is that a player of significant ability has become something of a joke in his own land

failed ventures, and the cash he has made from selling his story to the tabloids has dwindled to nothing.

In a bizarre incident he forfeited £100,000 in Dover when drugs officers seized cash bound for Holland. McAvennie claims he was investing in a treasure trove diving expedition in the English Channel, an excuse which led to the Rangers player Ally McCoist nicknaming him 'Blackbeard the Pirate'.

After a convoluted sting operation he was accused but acquitted of possessing Class A drugs in Newcastle, where he moved when the consistent pressure of being Frank McAvennie drove him from Scotland.

He has found love again – inevitably with a blonde – and plans to marry. Some mornings he walks to Newcastle's training ground to watch players go through the motions, many of them rich sportsmen on with less natural talent than McAvennie.

Making of a catchphrase

Perhaps the saddest thing of all is that a player of significant ability has become something of a joke in his own land. He has only himself and incredible misfortune to blame.

When his career was on the wane, McAvennie was encouraged to open a franchise of the theme restaurant School Dinners, at which glamorous waitresses dressed in schoolgirl gear served grub to leering men. In the colourful lives of the unholy trinity this decision captured the comic collateral that their lives as football

stars guaranteed them.

At the launch of the restaurant, which was, of course, a failure, Frank was called away to attend to an interview. Running behind schedule he hurriedly returned to have his

photo taken with a group of waitresses. The girls had momentarily disappeared. So Frank uttered those immortal lines, words that now come so easily to the lips of every living Scot.

All he said was "Where's The Burdz?"

He only said it once but it stuck. A catchphrase that has haunted Frank McAvennie ever since and for that we must all take the blame. ◊

By 2001, Frank McAvennie had returned to the rigorous Love Street training regime

14

WE'RE ON THE MARCH WITH WHITE STILETTOS

In the dark ages, before Hampden Babylon spread its scandalous stories across the park like manure, football fans huddled together like refugees, flat caps shielded their eyes and woodbine stained their fingers.

The noise in the old days was deafening and filled the smoked-out skies above industrial Scotland. By the Sixties their numbers had dwindled and they now leaned against fortified steel, wearing knitted hats and scarves, and waved strange wooden contraptions like dervishes.

By the last few years of the twentieth century their numbers had declined further and they were reluctantly directed along strictly defined rows, into plastic tip-up seats. Their noise was sporadic, even orchestrated, but it could barely be heard above public announcements, the crackling adverts and Tina Turner's *Simply the Best*. A black woman from Nutbush City Limits finally silenced the massed ranks of Scottish football.

Like nostalgia, being a fan is not what it used to be. While words like passion, loyalty and even fanaticism still describe the behaviour of some football fans, the act of being a spectator has changed profoundly.

In the woodbine days, football fans were in every key respects a mass. Local butchers stood out from the crowd and often saved up enough money from making mince pies to buy their local club. But the vast majority of fans shared a similar faith – they came to matches on a Saturday from the mills, the shipyards and the bonded warehouses. Football was a mass spectator sport.

Today the business of football is marked by the polarisation of rich and poor. And this trend, more than any other, will determine the future of the football fan. When Rangers signed Tore Andre Flo for £12m, not only was he the first Tore to be spotted in Scotland since Nicholas Fairbairn died, he cost more money than the entire turnover of the teams outside the SPL.

Flo's arrival in Scotland underlined the divide between rich and poor – only Rangers could afford to lavish that kind of money on a man who can trap a ball further than most players can kick it.

Money matters. Hard-core Rangers fans dig deeper into their resources to

"When I grow up, I'll be able to watch this crap on telly." A young Clyde fan before money talked

pay for season tickets, debentures and shares in the club. To remain loyal to the cause they are directed to an online emporium where you can own a quilted headboard with Barry Ferguson's autograph.

When we use the word 'fan' in 2001 we have to clarify whether we mean a consumer or a survivalist. Rangers fans are largely consumers. They face the prospect of buying digital smart cards which will provide entry to Ibrox via an electronic turnstile while Airdrie fans face simple oblivion.

Diamonds are forever?

Airdrie's loyal supporters once bathed their feet in vinegar, having walked the 17 long miles to an away game in Falkirk to raise sponsorship to pay the players wages. With the official receiver KPMG calling the shots and wannabe owner Steve Archibald searching the bargain bins of Spain for a squad of players willing to live in bedsits in Coatbridge, times were tight down Airdrie way.

But diamonds are a girl's best friend. Many of the bedraggled army of marchers that helped to save the club were women – supporters from darkest Lanarkshire willing to walk for Airdrie. To this day the sight of 300 Amazons wearing white stilettos and shellsuits is etched in the minds of passing motorists. Passion doesn't come more polarised – or more implausible – than that.

As a society we have never been more wealthy, but curiously we are also more inspired by bargains, by value and by the willingness to complain when goods or services are sub-standard. Football is not immune from these trends.

In 1999 Celtic fans boycotted the club's hooped shirts when it was discovered they disintegrated in your hands and bizarrely were made from a coloured dye that made rare frogs impotent. In the SPL, Dundee United's campaign-group United for Change has engaged in a long and bitter campaign to secure better fan representation on the Tannadice board. Such is the simmering resentment that then United manager Paul Sturrock briefly threatened to resign, claiming a sector of the United support were now damaging the club that had been the pride of Scotland in the 1980s.

The United fans maintained that Jim McLean's control of the club was driving it into the ground. For the first time in recent memory United existed in the shadow of their city rivals Dundee. This local spat reached its height in 2000 when McLean dramatically retired after banjoing a BBC journalist John Barnes. Meanwhile Dundee went on a spending spree attracting first a Bosnian warlord and a string of continental players to Dens.

As Dundee fans fawned at their new foreign stars, the Arabs watched a weekly nativity of donkeys and asses. The fans tried to wrestle back control of their club.

Fan Power

Over the last ten years there has been a slow but perceptible growth in the phenomenon of football fans organising themselves against their own club. The rise of oppositional spectatorship has its roots in the fanzine movement of the 1980s, when fans used satirical and scurrilous magazines to lampoon their own club. The most popular targets were rival clubs, arrogant players and

To this day the sight of 300 Amazons wearing white stilettos and shellsuits is etched in the minds of passing motorists

most importantly the club chairman.

Fanzines provided the forum for alternative approaches to football and became the ballast for the independent football fan movement, which sought to gain more fan representation on the board of football clubs. Football hooliganism, crowd disasters at Bradford and Hillsborough and the Taylor Report, which in turn brought about the all-seater stadium, created a significant shift in attitude.

Voice of the nation

In a sense this was football suffrage; for the first time in the history of the game football fans gained an official political voice.

In past seasons, Morton and Clydebank fans have engaged in sustained political campaigns to bring a semblance of order back to the clubs they love. Clydebank fans waged an urban guerrilla war that has led to boycotts, public stunts and to a fan handcuffing himself to the goal posts.

Being a football fan in the 21st century is destined to bring more change and greater polarisation in the fortunes of football clubs and their fans. At the very highest level, being a fan will become an act of 'virtual' support. Fans will watch on pay television, via glossy club magazines and through commercial websites. Owning the replica shirt will be the closest most fans will get to their passion.

Further down the food chain, among the soccer underclass, small groups of fans will cling to the past like soot on an ageing lung, trying to hold on to their history.

Some will face the stark choice between amalgamation, merger or compromise. In that scenario fanaticism will win and some fans will feel justified in driving the club they love into oblivion.

This is football's final solution and Babylon will tear its hanging gardens down. ◊

Approaching gloom

The financial foundations of Scottish football have never looked so precarious. Europe has all but abandoned the transfer system – once the lifeline of smaller clubs – and the inflationary spiral of players' wages puts even the most ordinary midfielder out of the price range of many clubs.

Ironically in the same week as Airdrie lurched closer to oblivion, the financial bible *Investor's Chronicle* devoted its columns to Scottish football under the sobering category of 'smaller companies'. It does not make for happy reading.

Season 2000–01 was not the happiest for Rangers fans for many reasons. Despite a jump in ticket sales and TV rights from their Champions' League campaign, the club registered a pre-tax loss of £25 million.

By far the biggest drain on Rangers' resources is players' wages or what the money men call 'amortisation', although the word 'dud' is easier to pronounce. It doesn't take a degree in accountancy to work out how Rangers' Profit and Loss account could have found a better stability – the names Negri, Prodan, Kanchelskis and Flo spring easily to mind.

Hearts' annual report makes even drearier reading. By the club's admission, the £8 million received from the Scottish Media Group has not yet produced "the move to the next level".

That is one of life's great understatements. Hearts' annual report revealed a £3.6 million loss and again players' wages are a significant drain. But the real sickener comes in a column devoted to player sales. The season before, Hearts had generated £1.48 million offloading the likes of David Weir and Paul Ritchie. In the last financial year, with the Bosman ruling in full effect, the club generated a paltry 53 grand on transfer fees. One-off transfers, such as the sale of Colin Cameron to Wolves, might help, but it isn't a long-term solution.

Celtic's latest published annual report would wipe the smile from the faces of even the club's most smug fans. Despite huge home crowds, the club still has a disappointingly low turnover – most Glasgow supermarkets take more money over the counter. The punters who turn up religiously every second Saturday do not provide anything like the revenue Celtic need to become a more substantial club to challenge the best clubs in Europe.

Significantly, the club's chairman warned shareholders that in the absence of significant new revenue streams, Celtic would have to sell players to help balance the books.

The message is clear: if you can stomach debt and don't mind your club living way beyond its means, then Scottish football has never been healthier. If you are an accountant turn the gas mark to nine and breathe deeply.

> **By far the biggest drain on Rangers' resources is players' wages or what the money men call 'amortisation', although the word 'dud' is easier to pronounce.**

STUART COSGROVE
A LIFE IN PHOTOS

❶ The author, on board a boat in Acapulco Bay, celebrates Scotland's doomed progress in the World Cup in Mexico. His pal, Tam Ower (right) advocates a healthy breakfast of two fags and a bottle of beer.

❸ After their escape from the FBI, Scotland fans try to sook-up to the Mexican polis. (From left: Mike Mason, Stan Harris, Geordie Jack, the polis and the author.)

❺ The author and Tam Ower check into rehab on their way to a Saints game at Celtic Park.

❷ Cosgrove celebrates St Johnstone's return to Premier League football at a special launch night for the first edition of *Hampden Babylon*, a book that has graced bargain bins throughout Scotland.

❹ At last it's Europe. Cosgrove photographs a group of ageing Saints fans on their way to a UEFA Cup match against VPS Vaasa of Finland. Remarkably these men have fought through two World Wars and the Great Depression to see their team in Europe. (From left: Mike Mason's dad George, Jim Kane, father of Saints captain Paul, and the author's uncle, Willie Cosgrove. Far right, proudly draped in a Saints scarf, is Murdo McLeod. At last we know who he really supports.)

❻ Scotland in Paris. Cosgrove joins Saints casuals, the Mainline Baby Squad, under the Eiffel Tower. The casuals are in their early twenties. Cosgrove is by now 68.